Open Education im Kontext
der Digitalisierung

Olaf Zawacki-Richter & Marco Kalz (Hrsg.)

Open Education im Kontext der Digitalisierung

Zeitschrift für Hochschulentwicklung
Jg. 14 / Nr. 2 (August 2019)

Impressum

**Zeitschrift für Hochschulentwicklung
Jg. 14 / Nr. 2 (August 2019)**

Open Education im Kontext der Digitalisierung

herausgegeben vom Verein Forum Neue Medien in der Lehre Austria

Graz, 2019

Herausgeber
Olaf Zawacki-Richter & Marco Kalz

ISBN
9783749467402

Herstellung und Verlag
BoD- Books on Demand, Norderstedt

Inhalt

Vorwort 7

Editorial: Open Education im Kontext der Digitalisierung 9
   Olaf Zawacki-Richter, Marco Kalz

Exploring OER Awareness and Engagement of Academics
from a Global South Perspective – a Case Study from Ghana 15
   Frank Senyo Loglo, Olaf Zawacki-Richter

Open Education Austria – ein Modell für die Integration von OERs
in die österreichischen Hochschulen 43
   Sylvia Lingo, Paolo Budroni, Raman Ganguly, Charlotte Zwiauer

Innovation through distance: The foundation of a satellite campus
and its implication on teaching activities in a STEM subject.................59
   Thomas Baumgartner

Digitale Transformation in Hochschulen: auf dem Weg
zu offenen Ökosystemen 85
   Sabine Seufert, Josef Guggemos, Luca Moser

Openness als Prinzip von Organisationsentwicklung. Werkbericht
zu partizipationsorientierten Dialogformaten im Projekt OERlabs........109
   Christian Helbig, Bence Lukács

Flip the Seminar – Digitale Vorbereitung auf Praxisphasen im Lehramt.............123
   Fabian Schumacher, Claudia Mertens, Melanie Basten

Vorwort

Als wissenschaftliches Publikationsorgan des Vereins Forum Neue Medien in der Lehre Austria kommt der Zeitschrift für Hochschulentwicklung besondere Bedeutung zu. Zum einen, weil sie aktuelle Themen der Hochschulentwicklung in den Bereichen Studien und Lehre aufgreift und somit als deutschsprachige, vor allem aber auch österreichische Plattform zum Austausch für Wissenschafter/innen, Praktiker/innen, Hochschulentwickler/innen und Hochschuldidaktiker/innen dient. Zum anderen, weil die ZFHE als Open-Access-Zeitschrift konzipiert und daher für alle Interessierten als elektronische Publikation frei und kostenlos verfügbar ist.

Es werden ca. 8.700 Artikel pro Monat geladen. Das zeigt die hohe Beliebtheit und Qualität der Zeitschrift sowie auch die große Reichweite im deutschsprachigen Raum. Gleichzeitig hat sich die Zeitschrift mittlerweile einen fixen Platz unter den hundert besten deutschsprachigen Wissenschaftspublikationen laut Google Scholar Metrics gesichert.

Dieser Erfolg ist einerseits dem international besetzten Editorial Board sowie den wechselnden Herausgeberinnen und Herausgebern zu verdanken, die mit viel Engagement dafür sorgen, dass jährlich mindestens vier Ausgaben erscheinen. Andererseits gewährleistet das österreichische Bundesministerium für Wissenschaft, Forschung und Wirtschaft durch seine kontinuierliche Förderung das langfristige Bestehen der Zeitschrift. Im Wissen, dass es die Zeitschrift ohne diese finanzielle Unterstützung nicht gäbe, möchten wir uns dafür besonders herzlich bedanken.

Das vorliegende Themenheft „Open Education im Kontext der Digitalisierung" will insbesondere die Verbindung zwischen Open Education und Digitalisierung herstellen. Dabei wird Open Education nicht auf Open Educational Resources oder das Lernen und Lehren mit digitalen Medien in einem engeren Sinne reduziert, sondern als Praxis und Initiativen in der Hochschulbildung verstanden, die auf die Öffnung der Wege zum und im Studium zielt. Die sechs veröffentlichten Beiträge bieten auf unterschiedlichen Ebenen Anknüpfungspunkte für die Forschung und Praxis.

Seit der Ausgabe 9/3 ist die ZFHE auch in gedruckter Form erhältlich und beispielsweise über Amazon beziehbar. Als Verein Forum Neue Medien in der Lehre Austria freuen wir uns, das Thema „Hochschulentwicklung" durch diese gelungene Ergänzung zur elektronischen Publikation noch breiter in der wissenschaftlichen Community verankern zu können.

In diesem Sinn wünschen wir Ihnen viel Freude bei der Lektüre der vorliegenden Ausgabe!

Martin Ebner und Hans-Peter Steinbacher
Präsidenten des Vereins Forum Neue Medien in der Lehre Austria

Olaf ZAWACKI-RICHTER[1](Oldenburg) & Marco KALZ (Heidelberg)

Editorial: Open Education im Kontext der Digitalisierung

Mit der enormen Verbreitung digitaler Medien, Tools und Endgeräte hat auch die Open Education (OE) Bewegung in der letzten Dekade an Fahrt aufgenommen (DEIMANN, 2019). Massive Open Online Courses (MOOCs) und Open Educational Resources (OER) sind aktuelle und im Rampenlicht stehende Erscheinungsformen dieser Entwicklung, die jedoch weit zurückreicht zur Idee des „Open Learning" (vgl. PETER & DEIMANN, 2012). Zugang zu höherer Bildung für nicht-traditionelle Zielgruppen zu eröffnen, ist die *raison d'être* der Open Universities, die schon immer Medien eingesetzt haben, um raum-zeitlich flexible Bildungsangebote zu schaffen (TAIT, 2008; XIAO, 2018).

Das Lernen und Lehren mit digitalen Medien ist nun (nicht nur) an Hochschulen durch die aktuell intensiv geführte Diskussion um die Digitalisierung noch weiter in den Mittelpunkt gerückt. Heute setzen mehr oder weniger alle Hochschulen digitale Medien in der Lehre ein. Einige Hochschulen haben digitale Lehre auch als strategisch relevantes Feld erkannt (GETTO & KERRES, 2017), um ihr Profil mit innovativer Lehre im grundständigen Bereich, als „offene Hochschule" (z. B. mit Blended-Learning-Angeboten für berufstätige Studierende) oder mit internationalen Online-Studiengängen zu schärfen.

Vor dem Hintergrund dieser dynamischen Entwicklung haben wir uns entschlossen, dieses Heft in der ZFHE zum Thema „Open Education im Kontext der Digitalisierung" herauszugeben, um insbesondere die Verbindung zwischen OE und Di-

---

[1] E-Mail: olaf.zawacki.richter@uni-oldenburg.de

gitalisierung herzustellen. Dabei wird OE nicht auf OER oder das Lernen und Lehren mit digitalen Medien in einem engeren Sinne reduziert, sondern OE ist weiter gefasst. Unter OE verstehen wir eine Praxis und Initiativen in der Hochschulbildung, die auf die Öffnung der Wege zum und im Studium zielt. Der Zugang zum Studium wird durchlässiger über Möglichkeiten des Zugangs auch ohne Abitur und die Anrechnung von hochschulisch und auch außerhochschulisch (formell und informell) erworbenen Kompetenzen und Qualifikationen (vgl. CONRAD, 2011). Digitale Medien werden genutzt, um raum-zeitlich flexible Angebote für Studierende weltweit zu schaffen. Dabei werden frei verfügbare und veränderbare Lernmaterialien, Tools und Systeme genutzt.

Zur Strukturierung der verschiedenen Fragestellungen und Aspekte von OE im Kontext der Digitalisierung ziehen wir ein weit rezipiertes Modell heran, das für das Feld von *Open and Distance Learning* von ZAWACKI-RICHTER (2009) und ZAWACKI-RICHTER & ANDERSON (2014) entwickelt wurde und drei große Forschungslinien beschreibt:

- Die Makro-Ebene oder globale Systemebene, auf der Aspekte ganzer Bildungssysteme, der Internationalisierung und des gleichberechtigten und durchlässigen Zugangs zur Hochschulbildung behandelt werden,

- die Meso-Ebene oder institutionelle Ebene des Bildungsmanagements, auf der Fragen der Organisations- und Personalentwicklung, der Angebotsentwicklung, des Innovations- und Qualitätsmanagements und der institutionellen Supportsysteme und Infrastruktur bearbeitet werden und

- die Mikro-Ebene des Lernens und Lehrens mit digitalen Medien, die Aspekte des didaktischen Designs, der Adressatenforschung und individueller Lern- und Lehrprozesse betrifft.

Sechs Beiträge konnten für dieses Themenheft ausgewählt werden, die sich wie folgt den drei oben genannten Ebenen zuordnen lassen:

Auf der Makro-Ebene geben *Frank Senyo Loglo und Olaf Zawacki-Richter* einen Einblick in das Hochschulsystem von Ghana, in dem der Zugang und die Nutzung frei verfügbarer Lern- und Lehrressourcen (OER) eine weitaus größere Bedeutung hat als in Ländern des globalen Nordens. Auf der Grundlage einer Fallstudie an einer großen TU mit mehreren Zweigstellen im ganzen Land werden die Einstellung der Lehrenden zu und deren Nutzung von OER untersucht. Eine wichtige Rolle spielt hier die wahrgenommene Qualität der Lernmaterialien und die Reputation der Institutionen, die die Materialien zur Verfügung stellen.

Der Werkstattbericht von *Sylvia Lingo, Paolo Budroni, Raman Ganguly und Charlotte Zwiauer* beschreibt das Projekt „Open Education Austria" (OEA), in dem es ebenfalls um OER geht – hier um die Erstellung, Bereitstellung und Verbreitung von OER in einem Portal für die Hochschulen in Österreich. Die Ergebnisse und Erfahrungen sind wertvoll auch für andere Systeme (etwa in Deutschland), die vor ganz ähnlichen Aufgaben zur Förderung von OER stehen.

Im Beitrag von *Thomas Baumgartner*, der sich auf der Meso-Ebene befindet, wird die räumliche Erweiterung und Öffnung des akademischen Angebotes einer Hochschule über einen sogenannten „Sattelite Campus" beschrieben. Diese Innovation stellt die Lehrenden und Mitarbeiter/innen vor Herausforderungen, die über die gezielte Nutzung von digitalen Medien und einen systematischen Innovationsprozess adressiert werden. Der Autor weist darauf hin, dass bei technologiegestützten Bildungsinnovationen in Hochschulen eine Integration von Top-down- und Bottom-up-Prozessen notwendig ist.

Auf der institutionellen Meso-Ebene beschäftigen sich *Sabine Seufert, Josef Guggemos und Luca Moser* mit der digitalen Transformation der Hochschulen und bringen hier den Ansatz „offener Lernökosysteme" für eine Organisations- und Hochschulentwicklung im digitalen Wandel ein. Das Ökosystem-Konzept bietet eine ganzheitliche Sichtweise auf die Beteiligung und Selbstorganisation der Akteurinnen und Akteure an Hochschulen, um das „Lernökosystem" gemeinsam weiter zu entwickeln. Besonders wird hier die Offenheit für eine Verbindung von formalem, non-formalem und informellem Lernen hervorgehoben.

Im Werkstattbericht von *Christian Helbig und Bence Lukács* werden OERLabs als offenes und dialogorientiertes Format vorgestellt, in dem durch das Ineinandergreifen von offener Kommunikation, Kollaboration und Einsatz von digitalen Medien offene Bildungspraktiken in Hochschulen realisiert werden können. Die Autoren konkludieren, dass Offenheit in der Bildung nicht nur als bildungsphilosophisches Projekt zu verstehen ist, sondern dass darin Prinzipien eingelagert sind, die für die Hochschul- bzw. Organisationsentwicklung eine wichtige Bedeutung haben.

Der Beitrag von *Fabian Schumacher, Claudia Mertens und Melanie Basten* diskutiert auf der Mikro-Ebene die Öffnung eines konkreten Lehrangebotes über ein Inverted-Classroom-Konzept. Das didaktische Design der Maßnahme und die Nutzung von Prinzipien der Offenheit im Sinne von Open Educational Resources und Open Educational Practices werden vorgestellt. Im Rahmen eines Seminars zum forschungsbasierten Lernen in den Praxisphasen der Lehramtsausbildung werden über ein Experimentaldesign die motivationalen Effekte der Maßnahme untersucht. Die Teilnehmenden der Intervention nehmen dabei eine bessere soziale Eingebundenheit wahr, während andere motivationale Dimensionen keine Unterschiede aufzeigen.

Als Gastherausgeber dieses Themenheftes wünschen wir Ihnen auch im Namen aller beteiligten Autorinnen und Autoren, dass die hier veröffentlichten Arbeiten Anknüpfungspunkte für Ihre Forschung und Praxis bieten und dass sie einen Beitrag zu einer verbindenden Sichtweise von OE und Digitalisierung leisten.

Olaf Zawacki-Richter und Marco Kalz
Oldenburg und Heidelberg, 5. August 2019

4 Literaturverzeichnis

Conrad, D. (2011). The landscape of prior learning assessment: A sampling from a diverse field. *International Review of Research in Open and Distance Learning*, *12*(1), 1-4.

Getto, B. & Kerres, M. (2017). Akteurinnen/Akteure der Digitalisierung im Hochschulsystem: Modernisierung oder Profilierung? *Zeitschrift für Hochschulentwicklung*, *12*(1), 123-142.

Peter, S. & Deimann, M. (2013). On the role of openness in education: A historical reconstruction. *Open Praxis*, *5*(1). https://doi.org/10.5944/openpraxis.5.1.23

Tait, A. (2008). What are open universities for? *Open Learning*, *23*(2), 85-93. https://doi.org/10.1080/02680510802051871

Xiao, J. (2018). On the margins or at the center? Distance education in higher education. *Distance Education*, 1-16. https://doi.org/10.1080/01587919.2018.1429213

Zawacki-Richter, O. (2009). Research areas in distance education – a Delphi study. *International Review of Research in Open and Distance Learning*, *10*(3), 1-17.

Zawacki-Richter, O. & Anderson, T. (Hrsg.) (2014). *Online distance education – towards a research agenda*. http://www.aupress.ca/index.php/books/120233

Herausgeber

Prof. Dr. Olaf ZAWACKI-RICHTER || Universität Oldenburg, Centre for Open Education Research (COER) & Centre for Lifelong Learning (C3L) || D-26129 Oldenburg

https://uol.de/coer/

olaf.zawacki.richter@uni-oldenburg.de

Prof. Dr. Marco KALZ || Pädagogische Hochschule Heidelberg, Institut für Kunst, Musik und Medien || Im Neuenheimer Feld 561, D-69120 Heidelberg

www.marcokalz.de

kalz@ph-heidelberg.de

Frank Senyo LOGLO[1] & Olaf ZAWACKI-RICHTER (Oldenburg)

Exploring OER Awareness and Engagement of Academics from a Global South Perspective – a Case Study from Ghana

Abstract

This study explored how academics in a Ghanaian university conceptualized and engaged with OER through a qualitative approach (in-depth interviews). "Access" emerged as the most dominant theme in how OER was conceptualized. Academics regarded OER positively; emphasizing its role in reducing the knowledge imbalances between the Global North and Global South and enhancing academic practices. Whilst some quality concerns about OERs were expressed, the reputation of sharing-institutions turned out as a significant factor in determining quality of the materials. Overall, the study revealed a deep-seated culture and practice of (re)use, revise, remix and redistribution of e-resources – akin to open practices, only that, this occurred locally among faculty, and at highly informal levels without the application of relevant open licences due to low awareness. In effect, the existing practices among faculty signal open-readiness.

Keywords

Open Educational Resources, OER awareness, OER engagement, Higher Education, Global South

---

[1] email: frank.senyo.loglo@uni-oldenburg.de

Scientific Contribution · DOI: 10.3217/zfhe-14-02/02

1   Introduction

Open Educational Resources (OER) have been suggested as a means of delivering access to higher education through the creation and sharing of learning resources (ATKINS, BROWN & HAMMOND, 2007; BEETHAM, FALCONER, MCGILL & LITTLEJOHN, 2012), and also seen as an attempt to correct the imbalances of quality education between the Global North and the Global South (UNESCO, 2015). Unfortunately, however, evidence of the promise of openness, and in particular, OERs to democratize and make education equitable and accessible to all learners around the world is inconclusive (ROLFE, 2017; WELLER, 2014).

Despite the implementation of a number of locally and externally driven OER initiatives within the Global South, BOZKURT, KOSEOGLU & SINGH (2019), KANWAR, BALSUBRAMANIAN, & UMAR (2010), KING, PEGRUM & FORSEY (2018) found the Global South and particularly Sub-Saharan Africa (SSA) to be consumers rather than producers regarding OER scholarship, open educational practice (OEP) and the creation and sharing of learning resources. This generally mirrors the trend in educational technology research (BOND, ZAWACKI-RICHTER & NICOLS, 2019). The underlying issue of inadequate technology infrastructure and low internet bandwidth, which have been long-standing barriers to OER adoption in the Global South, continue to linger (MTEBE & RAISAMO, 2014). This made BUTCHER (2015) advocate for a high percentage of learning resources to be shared as printable resources.

Despite the global and regional efforts towards mainstreaming OER in HEIs, its level of engagement, particularly among faculty members were found to be relatively low in previous studies (REED, 2012; ROLFE, 2012; SAMZUGI & MWINYIMBEGU, 2013). However, in light of recent digitization in HE delivery which has spurred an increase in access to global information, understanding the awareness of, and engagement with OER by faculty becomes essential. Even more so, a clearer picture of OER awareness and engagement among faculty in institutional contexts that are yet to implement any formal OER initiative provides a basis for a nuanced description and a barometer for the extent to which the OER movement permeates H.E in the Global South. Researching into the lived experiences of faculty who are users of digital learning resources -which may possibly include OER- could generate insights into the complex intersection of access, perception and engagement in a context with major structural constraints.

Thus, the study explored the level of OER awareness and the OER engagement levels among faculty members in a Ghanaian University.

In this regard, the following questions emerged and led the investigation of this topic:

1. What is the shared understanding of the concept of OER among the academic fraternity at Ghana TU?
2. What are faculty members' perceptions regarding OER in relation to academic practice?
3. What are the major OER engagement levels among academics of Ghana TU?

2 Theoretical Considerations

2.1 Open educational resources (OER) and their adoption

A universal construction of the concept of "openness" remains a subject of debate (WILEY, BLISS & McEWEN, 2014; WELLER, JORDAN, DE VRIES & ROLFE, 2018), resulting in varied interpretations in terms of scope (BAKER, 2017) and span of adoption (WELLER, 2014). In ROLFE's (2017) view, a constant calibration of the definition of "openness" is critical as the activities of the open movement advances and diversifies.

The term "OER" first emerged from a UNESCO forum in 2002 as "the open provision of educational resources, enabled by information and communication technologies for consultation, use and adaptation by a community of users for non-commercial purposes". Since then, different authors (e.g. ATKINS et al., 2007;

GURELL & WILEY, 2008) have offered varying definitions, albeit agreeing largely on key underlying concepts such as licensing and the cost-free nature of the resource to the user.

According to the Hewlett Foundation[2], open educational resources include full courses, course materials, modules, textbooks, streaming videos, tests, software, and any other tools, materials, or techniques used to support access to knowledge. In light of the widening scope and evolution of the OER concept, open platforms, systems, and architectures (KOSEOGLU & BOZKURT, 2018) as well as MOOCs (BOGA & MCGREAL, 2014) are regarded as a progressive step in the evolution of OER.

Perhaps, the most widely accepted definition of OER is the one updated in 2015 by UNESCO:

> Open Educational Resources (OERs) are any type of educational materials that are in the public domain or introduced with an open license. The nature of these open materials means that anyone can legally and freely copy, use, adapt and re-share them. OERs range from textbooks to curricula, syllabi, lecture notes, assignments, tests, projects, audio, video and animation.[3]

Despite the growing importance of OER, navigating around its wide-ranging practices remains a challenge (WILEY et al., 2014). WILEY's (2014) 5Rs of openness – retain, re (use), revise, remix and redistribute – provides the guiding framework around which the use and development of OER revolves. Therefore, a basic knowledge of copyright and licensing permission such as the Creative Commons is fundamental to understanding OER.

---

[2] http://www.hewlett.org/programs/education-program/openeducational-resources

[3] http://www.unesco.org/new/en/communication-and-information/access-to-knowledge/open-educational-rsources/what-are-open-educational-resources-oers/ (accessed February 13, 2019)

Barriers to OER adoption manifest in different and varying contexts. Its importance is emphasized by a recent study (BOZKURT, KOSEOGLU & SINGH, 2019) which found "barriers in OER" emerging as the most prominent theme from a lexical analysis of OER research paper titles and abstracts. According to WILEY et al. (2013), the following themes summarize the barriers to OER use and adoption:

- The discovery problem (making OER easier to find)
- The sustainability problem (financially self-sustaining),
- The quality problem (the pervasive notion that free represents low quality)
- The localization problem (improving knowledge to adapt OER to different contexts)
- The remix problem (the lack of exercise of revise and remix permissions)

These findings are consistent with PERCY & VAN BELLE (2012) and more recently by SEAMAN & SEAMAN (2018), who cited a lack of awareness and a perceived lack of offering as the cause for the slow but steady growth in the uptake and adoption process of OER.

2.2 OER and higher education

The OpenCourseWare initiative by the Massachusetts Institute of Technology (MIT) is regarded as the springboard for the start of OER movement in the early 2000s. Following that, a number of initiatives (e.g. OpenCourseWare Consortium and Open Education Consortium), whose membership are largely made up of HEIs, have been established to sustain the OER movement by creating and sharing content in an effort towards mainstreaming OER in HEIs

McGILL et al. (2013) outlines five major motivations by UK universities in making materials freely available: (1) building reputation of individuals or institutions or communities, (2) improving efficiency, cost and quality of production (3) opening access to knowledge (4) enhancing pedagogy and the students' learning experience (5) building technological momentum.

By the use of open licenses, academic knowledge has widened due to fewer re-strictions, and education materials are now beyond the campus, giving further rele-vance to the Open University models (WELLER, 2014). In another university in the UK, benefits derived by faculty from using OER include timesaving, which allowed for more finer-points discussions on subjects with students (ROLFE, 2017). Faculty in a non-English instructional context also shared similar sentiments (KURELOVIC, 2016).

Regarding OER and students' performance, PAWLYSHYN, BRADDLEE, CAS-PER & MILLER (2013) reported a higher pass rate among students who used OER in maths courses compared to those who used traditional materials. HILTON III, FISCHER, WILEY & WILLIAMS (2016) on the other hand found associations between OER adoption by faculty and improvements in course throughput rates. Thus, OER is seen as crucial for the promotion of innovation and change in educa-tional practices (PITT, 2015). However, issues related to quality assurance of (open) learning materials are an area of major concern in university contexts (JUNG, SASAKI & LATCHEM, 2016).

2.3   OER in the Global South

The term "Global South" is a designation for developing countries usually charac-terized by low-income status, and experience political or cultural marginalization (DADOS & CONNELL, 2012). Global South is used in the context of this study with a restricted reference to regions and states in Sub-Saharan Africa (SSA).

The anxiety about the uptake and adoption of OER in the Global South is not a new phenomenon. Concerns for its upscale and impact (ATKINS et al., 2007), barriers regarding technology (MTEBE, 2014) and the need for localization (WILSON, 2008) have long been highlighted. Recently, the gap between the North and South, in terms of contribution to scientific scholarship (BOZKURT, KOSEOGLU & SINGH, 2019) and the unidirectional flow of knowledge regarding OER creation and dissemination (KING, PEGRUM & FORSEY, 2018; WELLER et al., 2018) has been a source of worry. Accordingly, it is settled that interest from the North in

OER, far exceeds interest from the South (KANWAR et al., 2010; BATEMAN, LANE & MOON, 2012).

Other studies have been critical of the situation, describing it as limiting local academic development and in effect, consolidating the "northern hegemony" (CZER-NIEWICZ et al., 2014). BORZKURT et al. (2019) wonder whether the goal for open education to lessen the digital divide could be achieved in the face of an "open divide" (p. 86).

Despite what may appear as a drawback for advancing the integration of the South into the open ecology, recent developments signal opportunities rather than distress. Firstly, the growth and increasing popularity of mobile devices, portend well for OER adoption. Rather than computers, mobile devices have been suggested as ideal for accessing and sharing educational resources (CONOLE, 2014). Secondly, the establishment of new open universities have been observed in the Global South (QAYYUM & ZAWACKI-RICHTER, 2018; ZAWACKI-RICHTER & QAYYUM, 2019), indicating an opportunity for the expandability of the adoption and use of OER.

Locally and externally driven OER initiatives have also increased in the last decade. For example, OER Africa, which collaborates with HEIs in the development and use of OERs to enhance teaching and learning, developed the Teacher Education in Sub-Saharan Africa (TESSA) project under the auspices of the South African Institute for Distance Education (SAIDE). Another is the OER@AVU project by the African Virtual University (AVU), and the School of Open project, being instrumental projects. In a study by PERCY & VAN BELLE (2012), African academics' attitude towards OER was seen as positive and they believed it added value to their work.

2.4 Levels of OER engagement

Beneath the veneer of open practices lies the level of awareness of OER practitioners, which informs their engagement levels. This study thus conceptualizes engagement through the lenses of WELLER (2014) and WILD (2012). OER engagement is discussed in the context of this study as involving awareness and knowledge in wide ranging practices by faculty related to the (re)use, revision, remixing, retention and sharing of OER under an open licence (WILEY et al., 2014). In essence, OER engagement levels describe a hierarchy of proficiency that people demonstrate in how they use OER, usually being a function of their level of awareness and understanding.

According to WELLER (2014), engagement with OER could fall into one of three categories: Primary, Secondary and Tertiary – representing varying degrees of explicit awareness and utilization of OER. WILD (2012) on the other hand, conceptualized engagement with OER to reflect adoption from three stages – Piecemeal, Strategic and Embedded – signifying a continuum of very low to optimal levels of engagement.

Table 1 shows a mapping of the WILD (2012) and WELLER (2014) models.

Table 1: Mapping of WELLER (2014) and WILD (2012) OER engagement levels

WELLER (2014)	WILD (2012)	KEY CHARACTERISTICS	AWARENESS AND ENGAGE- MENT LEVEL
Primary usage	Embedded use	Knowledgeable in open licences and use of OER is rooted in their practices	High
Secondary usage	Strategic use	Fair idea of open licences and use of OER is selective, so far as it aids innovation	Medium
Tertiary usage	Piecemeal use	Use of OER and other digital resources cannot be differentiated	Low

Faculty awareness of OER has been a subject of previous and recent studies. AL-LEN & SEAMAN (2014) found that 34% of college faculty members in the United States were aware of OER. Similarly, SEAMAN & SEAMAN (2018) reported that 46% of faculty were aware of OER compared to 34% in 2015. However, WILEY et al. (2014) cautions that, faculty awareness of the term OER does not ensure that they fully understand the ideas of open licensing, and the ability to reuse and remix content, which are central to the concept of OER.

3   Design and method

3.1   Research approach

The study utilized an exploratory research approach, which is appropriate for a study of this nature that is concerned with discovery and insight generation into faculty members' awareness and engagement levels with OER. According to SCHUTT (2012), social exploratory research involves the investigation of social phenomena without explicit expectations (p. 12). The aim of this study was not to provide the final and conclusive answers to research questions, but to explore, with varying levels of depth (SINGH, 2007) to inform future research direction.

3.2   Participants' selection and background

The study population was the entire academic staff of a university based in Ghana. The case university is a public campus-based university, founded in 2006, and runs both undergraduate and postgraduate programmes. The university is reputed for its rich international collaboration profile, and prides itself as a leading university in Ghana with a strong technological focus.

In all, 18 interviews were conducted across the three faculties of the university (Engineering, Business and Computing), library and the Center for Online Learning and Teaching (COLT) (see table 2). Respondents' experience at the HE level spans between 4 years and 15 years, representing a blend of experienced academic staff who have worked within an era of digital advancement.

Table 2: Distribution of study participants

FACULTY/SECTION	Deans	Head of Dept.	Lecturers	Sub Total
Engineering	1	1	1	3
Computing & Info Systems	1	2	3	6
Business	1	2	4	7
Library		1		1
COLT		1		1
TOTAL				18

Respondents interviewed were from diverse disciplines including Accounting & Finance, Management Sciences, Economics, Computing Sciences, Telecommunication and Computing Engineering, Information Studies and Communication Studies, of whom nine (9) were terminal degree holders.

3.3   Data collection and analysis

Semi-structured interviews were conducted in the month of January 2019, with special focus on: (1) understanding of OER, (2) perceptions of OER in relation to academic practice and (3) OER engagement practices (5Rs), with all interviews, recorded and transcribed.

In this study, a thematic analysis approach was utilized, which allowed transcribed data to be analysed by identifying themes and concepts important to the description of the phenomenon of interest (DALY, KELLEHEAR & GLIKSMAN, 1997).

Usually in thematic analysis, patterns and themes that emerge from the textual data become the categories for analysis. However, both implicit and explicit ideas were analysed in order to derive meaning (BRAUN & CLARKE, 2006).

Leximancer software, a text-mining tool, was used to identify core concepts and how they are related to each other (SMITH & HUMPHREYS, 2006) within the responses provided by academic staff regarding their understanding of the term OER, which addressed research question 1: "what is the shared understanding of OER among academics in Ghana TU?"

4 Results

4.1 RQ1: What is the shared understanding of the concept "OER" among members of the academic fraternity at Ghana TU?

To understand how the term "OER" is conceptualized among academic staff in the university, verbatim responses (n=18) to the question asked were transcribed and inputted into Leximancer software to generate a concept map as depicted in Figure 1.

The thematic summary reveals that, "access" (100% relative count) had the most mentions, followed by "learning" (78%), "internet" (44%) and "open" (44%). The two most prominent themes – "access" and "learning" – signifies a primary emphasis on the removal of barriers to enable equitable participation in a learning process. This found expression through the concepts *people, educational, material, available, free, resources, location.* The third theme, "internet" highlights the role internet technologies play in enabling both access to the resources and learning. The connections between the concepts *location, resources and internet* implicitly highlight the dimension of flexibility, which is a key affordance of the internet technology.

The quotes below illustrate a cross-section of respondents' understanding of the concept "OER"

"What comes to mind is that it is any learning material that is free, easily accessible by anybody who wants to access it and it is not restricted" – Lecturer W.

"Library Resources that are made available for people to access mostly for free under some permissions" – Head of Department.

"They could be journals, they could be books, they could be instructional materials that are online for anybody at all who has need for it to access and use for his benefit. If you write a book and put it online and put a password on it and ask me to pay before using it, then it is not open". – Lecturer B.

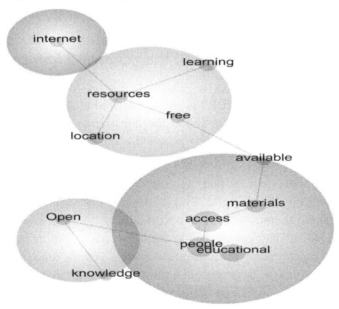

Figure 1: Concept map of the shared understanding of the term OER by faculty of Ghana TU.

4.2 RQ2: What are faculty members' perceptions regarding OER in relation to academic practice?

Perceptions regarding OER and its implications for the academic practice of respondents were mixed but mostly positive. The emerging themes from views expressed were categorized in the following contexts:

4.2.1 Facilitation of knowledge sharing and dissemination

This theme emerged and was viewed largely through the lenses of easy access to relevant learning resources particularly for people from deprived regions of the world. A Head of Department in explaining how OER in his view, facilitates knowledge sharing and dissemination, remarked:

"You know textbooks is an issue, bearing in mind we live in the developing world. We have a few but many of them are old so I advise lecturers to go online and look for updated materials".

"It is good in terms of sharing and knowledge dissemination. Luckily, somebody else has done it [developed learning resource] for you or aided you….why do you have to start it from scratch?" – Lecturer C.

In what he considered as a minor downside to the easy access to knowledge sharing, a Dean was of the view that:

"Some faculty members may take things for granted since they know they can always get materials, hence do not develop authentic materials of their own and always depend on others" – Dean A.

4.2.2 Improvement in educational practices

This theme's emergence espouses three key points related to how OER could improve the educational practice of faculty members who engage with OER. Firstly, faculty members who develop content get the opportunity to receive feedback in order to improve their resources. Secondly, there is an opportunity to benchmark with established scholars and institutions from other parts of the world. Thirdly, an enhanced reputation and high satisfaction, derived from knowing how far a resource developed by an academic reaches. A lecturer explained how his teaching methods are improving from using a free instructor manual from CENGAGE Publishers:

"For me I think it [free instructor manual] is good because, first, it acts as an instructor to you, before you go and instruct your class. It has really improved my teaching methods" – Lecturer F.

In terms of possible benefits that could be derived from peer review:

"It [OER] is very good, especially if you develop content and share, and people all over the world have the opportunity to provide feedback to help improve the content". – Lecturer P.

4.2.3 Quality and reputation of OER

The notion that OER are free and accessible anywhere made some respondents apprehensive regarding its quality. To some of the academics, the very good books and learning resources are mostly commercial and proprietary. These concerns were expressed as follows:

"When a book is very good and they want to use it as a textbook, the publishers want their money so they won't put it up for everybody to access...at best good open access books will only be used as reference books". – Library Respondent.

"It is just a fact of life that the best books must be paid for. Some free books are okay, but the best ones are mostly not free". – Lecturer M.

However, a Head of Department who held a contrary view, said as follows:

"When a resource is open, it does not make it inferior to the proprietary resources. In fact, some open resources and books are funded...and are of higher quality compared to proprietary textbooks because it goes through a rigorous academic review process". – Head of Department 4.

The source of an OER also emerged as an important indicator of quality. There were indications that, some shared content could be of questionable quality since content on the internet can be uploaded by anybody. Some of the respondents alluded to an inclination towards resources created by revered scholars and institutions, which provides assurance of the quality of the resource. The following quotes demonstrate how resources from highly reputable institutions are perceived:

"If a formidable university such as MIT [Massachusetts Institute of Technology] has developed materials and shared for free, why wouldn't you use it? This is MIT we are talking about. They will not just share anything because their reputation is at stake" – Lecturer P.

"For example, when I want to take an online course, I pay attention to the institutions offering the course before I go ahead [to sign up]. When it is from Harvard, Yale, Princeton etc…. you are sure to get the best [quality]. – Lecturer N.

4.3 RQ 3: What are the major OER engagement levels among academics of Ghana TU?

In assessing, the levels of OER engagement among faculty, activities and practices were examined with emphasis on awareness of OER through (re)use, discovery, creation and sharing practices.

4.3.1 OER Awareness among faculty of Ghana TU

The use of digital resources for teaching and learning were found to be widespread among faculty members interviewed. Among other things, resources such as presentation slides, lecture notes, videos, books, course materials and sample questions (sometimes with answers) were used to support teaching and learning. An important but unsurprising revelation was that, although many lecturers used a mix of media and resources, they could not distinguish between an ordinary free digital resource and OER. For some, it was their first time learning about the term "OER", while others considered any freely accessible resource on the internet as an open resource, which generally stemmed from their knowledge of open access. A quote from a lecturer captures this notion:

"For me once I am able to access a material online without having to pay any subscription or download fee, then it is an open access resource." – Lecturer T.

Whilst a few were familiar with the MIT Open Courseware and popular MOOC sites such as Coursera, OpenLearn, Lynda and edX, (most mentions), many however, did not conceptualize MOOCs within the context of OER.

Additionally, knowledge of open licenses was found to be very low, with the exception of three (3) respondents, predictably, majority of whom were affiliated with the Faculty of Computing and Information Systems. A Head of Department who had a very good understanding of the creative common licensing and its application said:

"...people think once a resource is openly shared, you lose control of ownership. Normally, the licensing regime gives you an indication of the type of permission given and the specific boundaries for use of the resource..." – Head of Department 4.

4.3.2 Content sharing and redistribution

Whilst it was clear that many of the respondents were not explicitly aware of OER, sharing of learning resources – print and digital – locally was common practice. No lecturer reported ever sharing a resource under an open licence, but rather, through informal means such as: peer sharing or passing it from senior academics to junior colleagues. A lecturer provided an account of how he and another colleague, teaching the same course, but to different class sections (morning and weekend), shared teaching resources. In addition, lecturers who were new to a particular course sometimes relied on materials developed by the previous course lecturer. Some respondents also indicated receiving and sharing instructional materials with colleagues from other universities but within the same field. It is instructive to note that the resources (presentation slides, lecture notes, test items) developed by the lecturers were not shared under any open licenses.

At a more formal level, mostly initiated by the Deans and Heads of Department, relevant resources are brought to the attention of faculty at meetings, or the links shared via the faculty-emailing list. Other faculties have instituted mentoring schemes for new lecturers to enable them fully integrate and adapt to the ethos of the faculty by sharing resources with them.

Below are what some respondents said of sharing practices:

"This semester for example, I am mentoring a new lecturer who has joined our faculty....so we are teaching a course I have taught before together, and I have given all my materials to him to help him develop his". – Dean B.

"For instance, I had to teach a new topic I had never taught before, so I contacted two lecturers who had taught it in the past. I took their lecture notes and test items and it served a good guide" – Lecturer O.

A lecturer who shared instances of how they direct students to various online resources to obtain materials to supplement their leaning had this to say:

"There is this site called "lynda.com" and "pdfdrive.net", ... I get materials from there myself, but I always ask students to go there to get additional resources to help them with further reading" – Lecturer T.

Notwithstanding, some lecturers download the resources (presentation slides, pdf, etc.) and share with students via the LMS or email. It also appeared to be a common practice to share links via WhatsApp messenger. Occasional photocopies of books are made, particularly of books whose e-versions were not available.

4.3.3 Resource discovery and acquisition

Typically, faculty members discovered digital resources through referrals from colleagues or by simply exploring the internet through search engines or from specific MOOC sites. The university's library shares links to digital resources for use by academic staff. In the case of e-books, they are either purchased online or downloaded at no cost. Furthermore, some faculty members have signed up to commercial publishers (eg. CENGAGE, Pearson and Wiley) and occasionally receive free instructor manuals, presentation slides and evaluation copies of textbooks for their use.

In what appears to be a call for greater use of library resources, the Librarian said:

"Accessing open resources through the library is better than just ordinary google search"

The rationale for such line of thought was that, the library staff, who are professionals, were better equipped to collate the best OER, relevant to the disciplines of the academics.

Similarly, the Centre for Online Teaching and Learning (COLT) has provided links to e-resources on its website and linked the LMS to the university's e-library system. Unfortunately, however, the patronage of such resources were observed to be very low. Reasons provided included: (1) some faculty members belonged to professional bodies (e.g. IEEE) and rather preferred to utilize those resources; (2) some faculty who are/were studying abroad have access to libraries from their universities and still use them. Although faculty who fall under the scenarios described may be in the minority, it is believed they share these resources with colleagues.

Nevertheless, a number of lecturers still purchase printed books when the e-versions are not openly and freely accessible. While the university provides support in the form of book allowance (equivalent of $600 per academic year), the high cost of some books leads to the use of unapproved and unorthodox means of finding books hidden behind the paywalls of publishers. Two lecturers narrated their difficulties in accessing some resources online:

"From time to time, the library sends out links to some resources, but because we have to pay for some of them, we are unable to access it". – Lecturer W.

"Sometimes when I am not able to buy the book, I ask a friend who then goes online to look for a crack version to use. I know it is not right but without it, I cannot have access to some very good books". – Lecturer F.

On the possible repercussions of breaking copyright laws, a respondent remarked that:

"Some do it out of love and passion to learn, but others also do it out of ignorance. But the truth is that, as a developing country we get away with a lot of things we otherwise wouldn't if we were in a developed country" – Head of Department 3.

4.3.4 Revise and remix practices

The most common contents created by lecturers are course outlines, presentation slides, test questions and a few video contents. According to COLT, about 10 short videos have been shared on the centre's YouTube site. Majority of respondents also confirmed that they sometimes create content by relying on some resources found online. However, due to lecturers' limitations in the awareness and utilization of open licenses, most of the revise and remix activities are done unconsciously without applying any open licensing.

In shedding light on informal revise and remix practices, a lecturer said:

"I don't use them [digital resources found online] as I get them but I also use other resources to modify the contents to suit the needs of my students" – Lecturer S.

5   Discussion

Findings indicate that, "access" formed the key focus of faculty members' conceptualization of the term "OER". This perhaps accentuates their belief that learning resources and opportunities for learning, should be made available to all who wish to participate without any inhibition. Also evident was the fact that, allusions to *free* in the context of understanding OER represented (no) cost, and not in ways reflecting the freedom and choice a user has in adopting and utilizing OER (WELLER, 2014). A first-hand sense and interpretation of the thought processes of the academics regarding their collective understanding of OER as seen in the concept map represents access to materials for an activity (learning), which is undertaken at no cost (free) and enabled by a medium (internet) which makes the activity flexible (location). It was apparent that the role of technology in achieving the objectives of OER was clearly recognized.

In what appears to be a recurring theme of OER research, concepts related to licensing and copyright permissions were absent (e.g. ALLEN & SEAMAN, 2014; DE HART, CHETTY & ARCHER, 2015). Given that licensing determines the level of "openness" of a resource, knowledge of it is a precondition to the understanding of the concept of OER (WILEY et al., 2014). This situation transcends the Global South (DE LOS ARCOS & WELLER, 2018) therefore, a re-think in the advocacy strategies is required. Licencing and copyright issues should be put at the forefront in discourse of openness in order to deepen the concept of OER.

Interesting views were expressed regarding respondents' perception of OER on their academic practice. First, OER was perceived as a public good, and as such, knowledge must be shared and disseminated. However, the view was held that, people of the Global South stand to gain more from the public good, and this reflects OER's acclaim to be a means to increase access and provide quality learning resources to people in deprived regions (UNESCO, 2015).

Secondly, faculty members' perception of OER as an enabler for the improvement of their academic practice was telling. They believed this could be achieved through activities such as public peer review, peer scrutiny and benchmarking to improve pedagogical practices. This perhaps indicates a reflective recognition of how open practices could improve the quality of materials made available for use and adaptation for teaching and learning, which mirrors findings by ORR, RIMINI & VAN DAMME (2015), stressing the need for quality materials through OER.

Thirdly, the perception that "free" could connote inferior resources emerged quite strongly. This may possibly be due to long-standing familiarity with resources from commercial publishers, or a lack of capacity to evaluate the quality of an OER or perhaps, a discovery problem (WILEY et al., 2013; PERCY & VAN BELLE, 2012) where faculty are unable to locate discipline-relevant OER. It was also noteworthy that, resources shared by institutions considered as renowned, would most likely be held to a relatively lower standard of scrutiny by virtue of their reputation. The implication of this perception is that, knowledge flow in the North-South direction is expected to continue, given that more matured and better quality educational systems are located in the North.

The observation of pervasive use of digital resources for teaching and learning appeared to be a culture within the institution. Regardless, awareness of OER was low, with an overwhelming majority of faculty using a mix of media without necessarily being able to distinguish clearly between OER and other digital resources accessible on the internet, which are characteristics indicative of primary users (WELLER, 2014) or piecemeal users of OER (WILD, 2012).

Resources for teaching and learning were accessed from both internal and external sources. Although the library provided e-resources, kept on the university server, the majority of those accessed were from external sources, mainly through faculty exploration using search engines, or subscriptions with commercial publishers. It emerged that, many faculty members resorted to digging up alternative digital materials only when recommended books (mostly commercial) could not be accessed, generally because of high costs. These kinds of situations provide an incentive for people to gain access to copyrighted resources through illicit means. This is also suggestive of a deficiency in locating open textbooks, relevant for their subject areas. This is perhaps due to the absence of a community of practice, which emphasizes ELHERS & CONOLE's (2010) call for a focus on open educational practices in order to derive the full benefits from of OER.

The 5R principles – retain, reuse, revise, remix and redistribute – which underlie OER were abundantly seen in practice among faculty members, albeit locally and informally, without the application of relevant open licences. Despite that, these signs portend well for OER uptake.

6 Conclusion and implications for further research

The study addressed faculty members' shared understanding of OER and assessed their perception of same regarding their academic practice. Useful insights were gained from the study which has implications for OER adoption and use. First, "access" was the most fundamental consideration when conceptualizing OER among faculty of Ghana TU while the issue of licensing remained latent. Secondly, perceptions of OER were positive and mostly centred on the benefit the Southern users derived in terms of knowledge, improvement in the quality of resources through peer practices and regarding learning materials originating from institutions of repute to be of high quality. Thirdly, faculty use of digital resources are intense, however, there is a dearth in distinguishing OER from other ordinary or proprietary digital resources. Finally, OER engagement levels were found to be low and informal for the reason that, faculty created, reused, revised and redistributed digital resources with no open licences.

Despite the well-known structural obstacles facing the Global South in terms of OER adoption and use, the growing use of mobile devices provide practical and targeted pointers on reducing the "open divide". Additionally, collaborative research projects with Northern practitioners and deepening open educational practices at local levels through the deliberate creation of communities of practice are but a few strategies for promoting increased OER engagement.

Due to the sample size and the exploratory nature of the study, findings cannot be generalized to the population and must therefore be interpreted with caution. This study is the first step towards understanding OER engagement practices within a Southern institutional context yet to formally adopt OER. Future research will focus on a large scale study aimed at investigating opportunities for fostering open educational practices.

7 References

Allen, I. E., & Seaman, J. (2014). *Opening the curriculum: Open educational resources in U.S. higher education*. Retrieved from Babson Survey Research Group website: www.onlinelearningsurvey.com/oer.html

Atkinks, D. E., Brown, J. S., & Hammond, J. S. (2007). *A review of the open educational resources (OER) movement: Achievements, challenges, and new opportunities*. Retrieved from William and Flora Hewlett Foundation website: https://hewlett.org/wp-content/uploads/2016/08/ReviewoftheOERMovement.pdf

Baker, F. W. (2017). An alternative approach: Openness in education over the last 100 years. *TechTrends, 61*(2), 130-140. https://doi.org/doi.org/10.1007/s11528-016-0095-7

Bateman, P., Lane, A., & Moon, R. (2012). An emerging typology for analysing OER initiatives. *Cambridge 2012: Innovation and Impact – Openly Collaborating to Enhance Education*, 19-28. Retrieved from http://oro.open.ac.uk/33243/

Beetham, H., Falconer, I., McGill, L., & Littlejohn, A. (2012). *Open practices: Briefing paper [JISC]*. Retrieved from https://oersynth.pbworks.com/w/file/fetch/58444186/Open%20Practices%20briefing%20paper.pdf

Boga, S., & McGreal, R. (2014). *Introducing MOOCs to Africa: New economy skills for Africa program – ICT*. Retrieved from Commonwealth of Learning website: http://oasis.col.org/handle/11599/613

Bond, M., Zawacki-Richter, O., & Nichols, M. (2019). Revisiting five decades of educational technology research: A content and authorship analysis of the British Journal of Educational Technology. *British Journal of Educational Technology, 50*(1), 12-63. https://doi.org/10.1111/bjet.12730

Bozkurt , A., Koseoglu, S., & Singh, L. (2019). An analysis of peer reviewed publications on openness in education in half a century: Trends and patterns in the open hemisphere. *Australasian Journal of Educational Technology, 35*(4). https://doi.org/10.14742/ajet.4252

Braun, V., & Clarke, V. (2006). Using thematic analysis in psychology. *Qualitative Research in Psychology, 3*(2), 77-101. https://doi.org/10.1191/1478088706qp063oa

Butcher, N. (2015). *A basic guide to open educational resources (OER)* (Kanwar, A. & Uvalić-Trumbić, S, Eds.). Retrieved from https://unesdoc.unesco.org/ark:/48223/pf0000215804

Conole, G. (2014). The Use of Technology in Distance Education. In O. Zawacki-Richter, & T. Anderson (Eds.), *Online distance education: Towards a research agenda.* (pp. 217-236). AU Press.

Czerniewicz, L., Deacon, A., Small, J., & Waliji, S. (2014). Developing World MOOCs: A Curriculum View of the MOOC Landscape. *Journal of Global Literacies, Technologies, and Emerging Pedagogies, 2*(3), 122-139.

Dados, N., & Connell, R. (2012). The Global South. *Contexts, 11*(1), 12-13. https://doi.org/10.1177%2F1536504212436479

Daly, J., Kellehear, A., & Gliksman, M. (1998). *The Public Health Researcher: A Methodological Approach.* Melbourne: Oxford University Press.

de Hart, K., Chetty, Y., & Archer, E. (2015). Uptake of OER by staff in distance education in South Africa. *The International Review of Research in Open and Distributed Learning, 16*(2). https://doi.org/10.19173/irrodl.v16i2.2047

de los Arcos, B., Weller, M. (2018). A Tale of Two Globes: Exploring the North/South Divide in Engagement with Open Educational Resources. In J. Schöpfel, & U. Herb (Eds.), *Open Divide: Critical Studies on Open Access* (pp. 147-155). Retrieved from https://core.ac.uk/download/pdf/153444282.pdf

Elhers, U. D., & Conole, G. (2010, May). *Open educational practices: unleashing the power of OER.* Presented at the UNESCO Workshop on OER, Namibia. Retrieved from https://oerknowledgecloud.org/sites/oerknowledgecloud.org/files/OEP_Unleashing-the-power-of-OER.pdf

Gurell, S., & Wiley, D. (2008). *OER Handbook for Educators.* WikiEducator.

Hilton III, J., Fischer, L., & William, L. (2016). Maintaining Momentum Toward Graduation: OER and the Course Throughput Rate. *International Review of Research in Open and Distributed Learning*, *17*(6). https://doi.org/10.19173/irrodl.v17i6.2686

Jung, I., Sasaki, T., & Latchem, C. (2016). A framework for assessing fitness for purpose in open educational resources. *International Journal of Educational Technology in Higher Education*, *13*(1), 1-11. https://doi.org/10.1186/s41239-016-0002-5

Kanwar, A., Balasubramanian, K., & Umar, A. (2010). Toward sustainable open education resources: a perspective from the global south. *American Journal of Distance Education*, *24*(2), 65-80. https://doi.org/10.1080/08923641003696588

King, M., Pegrum, M., & Forsey, M. (2018). MOOCs and OER in the Global South: Problems and Potential. *International Review of Research in Open and Distributed Learning*, *19*(5). https://doi.org/doi.org/10.19173/irrodl.v19i5.3742

Koseoglu, S., & Bozkurt, A. (2018). An exploratory literature review on open educational practices. *Distance Education*, *39*(4), 441-461. https://doi.org/10.1080/01587919.2018.1520042

Kurelovic, K. E. (2016). Advantages and limitations of usage of open educational resources in small countries. *International Journal of Research in Education and Science (IJRES)*, *2*(1), 136-142.

McGill, L., Falconer, I., Dempster, J. A., Littlejohn, A., & Beetham, H. (2013). *Journeys to Open Educational Practice: UKOER/SCORE Review Final Report*. London: JISC.

Mtebe, J., & Raisamo, R. (2014). Investigating perceived barriers to the use of open educational resources in higher education in Tanzania. *International Review of Research in Open and Distributed Learning (IRRODL)*, *15*(2). https://doi.org/10.19173/irrodl.v15i2.1803

Orr, D., Rimini, M., & van Damme, D. (2015). *Open Educational Resources: A Catalyst for Innovation, Educational Research and Innovation*. Paris: OECD Publishing.

Pawlyshyn, N., Braddlee, D., Casper, L., & Miller, H. (2013, November). Adopting OER: A case study of cross-institutional collaboration and innovation. *Educause Review*. Retrieved from http://www.educause.edu/ero/article/adopting-oer-case-study-cross-institutional-collaboration-and-innovation

Percy, T., & Van Belle, J. P. (2012). Exploring the barriers and enablers to the use of open educational resources by university academics in Africa. *IFIP Advances in Information and Communication Technology Conference*, *378*, 112-128. Retrieved from http://dl.ifip.org/db/conf/oss/oss2012/PercyB12.pdf

Pitt, R. (2015). Mainstreaming Open Textbooks: Educator Perspectives on the Impact of OpenStax College Open Textbooks. *International Review of Research in Open and Distributed Learning*, *16*(4). https://doi.org/10.19173/irrodl.v16i4.2381

Qayyum, A., & Zawacki-Richter, O. (Eds.) (2018). *Open and Distance Education in Australia, Europe and the Americas: National Perspectives in a Digital Age* (Vol. 1). Retrieved from https://link.springer.com/book/10.1007%2F978-981-13-0298-5

Reed, P. (2012). Awareness, attitudes and participation of teaching staff towards the open content movement in one university. *Research in Learning Technology*, *20*. https://doi.org/10.3402/rlt.v20i0.18520

Rolfe, V. (2012). Open Educational Resources: Staff attitudes and awareness. *Research in Learning Technology*, *20*. https://doi.org/10.3402/rlt.v20i0.18520

Rolfe, V. (2017). Striving toward openness: But what do we really mean? *International Review of Research in Open and Distributed Learning (IRRODL)*, *18*(7), 75-88. https://doi.org/10.19173/irrodl.v18i7.3207

Samzugi, A. S., & Mwinyimbegu, C. M. (2013). Accessibility of Open Educational Resources for Distance Education learners: The case of the Open University of Tanzania. *Journal of The Open University of Tanzania*, *14*, 76-88.

Schutt, R. K. (2012). *Investigating the social world: The process and practice of research* (7th ed.). Thousand Oaks, CA: Sage.

Seaman, J. E, & Seaman, J. (2018). *Freeing the Textbook: Educational Resources in U.S. Higher Education*. Retrieved from Babson Survey Research Group website: https://www.onlinelearningsurvey.com/reports/freeingthetextbook2018.pdf

Singh, K. (2007). *Quantitative Social Research Methods*. New Delhi: Sage.

Smith, A. E., & Humphreys, M. S. (2006). Evaluation of unsupervised semantic mapping of natural language with Leximancer concept mapping. *Behavior Research Methods*, *38*(2), 262-279.

UNESCO, & Commonwealth of Learning (COL) (2011). *Guidelines for open educational resources (OER) in higher education*. Retrieved from https://unesdoc.unesco.org/ark:/48223/pf0000213605

Weller, M. (2014). *The Battle for Open: How openness won and why it doesn't feel like victory*. http://dx.doi.org/10.5334/bam

Weller, M., Jordan, K., DeVries, I., & Rolfe, V. (2018). Mapping the open education landscape: Citation network analysis of historical open and distance education research. *Open Praxis*, *10*(2), 109-126. https://doi.org/doi.org/10.5944/openpraxis.10.2.822

Wild, J. (2012). *OER Engagement Study: Promoting OER reuse among academics* [SCORE Research report.]. Retrieved from https://askawild.files.wordpress.com/2017/09/oer-engagement-study-joanna-wild_full-research-report.pdf

Wiley, D. (2014). Clarifying the 5th R. Iterating toward openness. Retrieved November 18, 2018, from http:// www.opencontent.org/blog/archives/3251

Wiley, D., Bliss, T. J., & McEwen, M. (2014). Open educational resources: A review of the literature. In *Handbook of research on educational communications and technology* (pp. 781-789). New York: Springer.

Wilson, T. (2008). New ways of mediating learning: Investigating the implications of adopting open educational resources for tertiary education at an institution in the United Kingdom as compared to one in South Africa. *International Review of Research in Open and Distributed Learning (IRRODL)*, *9*(1), 1-19. https://doi.org/doi.org/10.19173/irrodl.v9i1.485

Zawacki-Richter, O., & Qayyum, A. (Eds.) (2019). Open and Distance Education in Asia, Africa and the Middle East: National Perspectives in a Digital Age (Vol. 2). Singapore: Springer. Retrieved from https://www.springer.com/de/book/9789811357862

Authors

Frank Senyo LOGLO || University of Oldenburg, Centre for Open Education Research (COER) || 26129 Oldenburg, Germany

https://uol.de/coer

frank.senyo.loglo@uni-oldenburg.de

Prof. Dr. Olaf ZAWACKI-RICHTER || University of Oldenburg, Centre for Open Education Research (COER) & Centre for Lifelong Learning (C3L) || 26129 Oldenburg, Germany

https://uol.de/coer/

olaf.zawacki.richter@uni-oldenburg.de

Sylvia LINGO[1], Paolo BUDRONI, Raman GANGULY &
Charlotte ZWIAUER (Wien)

Open Education Austria – ein Modell für die Integration von OERs in die österreichischen Hochschulen

Zusammenfassung

Im Rahmen des Projekts „Open Education Austria" (OEA) wurde ein universitätsübergreifendes Fachportal für Open Educational Resources (OER) konzipiert und als Pilot realisiert. Zugleich wurden Services und Qualifizierungsangebote für Lehrende zur Entwicklung mehrfach nutzbarer OER etabliert (z. B. einsetzbar in Aufnahmeverfahren, Brückenkursen, Lehrveranstaltungen, Offenen Online-Kursen). Sowohl Portal als auch Services erfordern eine gezielte Bündelung von Expertisen von (E-)Learning-Zentrum, Bibliothek und Zentralem Informatikdienst. In diesem Beitrag werden das Projekt mit seinen Herausforderungen und bisherigen Ergebnissen, aber auch Lessons Learned zur Diskussion gestellt.

Schlüsselwörter

OER-Contententwicklung, OER-Fachportal, OER-Qualifizierung, OER-Strategie, Hochschulentwicklung

---

[1] E-Mail: sylvia.lingo@univie.ac.at

Werkstattbericht · DOI: 10.3217/zfhe-14-02/03

43

Open Education Austria – An Austrian model for OER integration in higher education

Abstract

As part of the project "Open Education Austria" (OEA), a cross-university-specific online portal for Open Educational Resources (OER) was designed and implemented as the initial implementation case. At the same time, services and qualification offerings for teachers were established for the development of reusable OER (e.g., use in admission procedures, bridging courses, courses, open online courses). Both the technical portal and the services for teachers required a focused pooling of (e-)learning centre expertise, libraries and central computer services. This paper discusses the project, including the challenges and previous results, as well as the lessons learned.

Keywords

OER content production, OER infrastructure, OER qualification & training, OER strategy, developments in higher education

1   Ausgangslage

Im Projekt „Open Education Austria" (finanziert über Hochschulraum-Strukturmittel 2016-2019, ausgeschrieben vom Bundesministerium für Wissenschaft und Forschung, Österreich) wurden von den beteiligten Universitäten schrittweise Services für Lehrende und ein Fachportal als Infrastruktur für Open Educational Resources (OER) erarbeitet. Dabei wurden erstmals inneruniversitäre Dienstleistungen von (E-)Learning-Zentren, Bibliotheken und Zentralen Informatikdiensten verknüpft und es erfolgte eine interuniversitäre Vernetzung zur Implementierung von OER. Im Fachportal können Lehrende ihre Lernobjekte nach dem Ownerprinzip als OER qualitätsgesichert (durch fachliche Beratung des Supportteams und Qualifizierungsangebote an den beteiligten Universitäten) für die Nachnutzung zur Verfügung stellen. Im Projektkonsortium sind die Universität Wien, die Technische Universität Graz, die Karl-Franzens-Universität Graz sowie die Universität Innsbruck vertreten. Der Beitrag ist insbesondere aus der Perspektive der Universität Wien (Projektleitung) und der hier etablierten Infrastrukturen verfasst.

2 Projektkontext

Die „Berliner Erklärung über den offenen Zugang zu wissenschaftlichem Wissen" von 2003[2] hat die Idee der freien Weitergabe von universitärem Wissen über das Internet nachhaltig geprägt: „Unsere Aufgabe Wissen weiterzugeben ist nur halb erfüllt, wenn diese Informationen für die Gesellschaft nicht in umfassender Weise und einfach zugänglich sind. Neben den konventionellen Methoden müssen zunehmend auch die neuen Möglichkeiten der Wissensverbreitung über das Internet nach dem Prinzip des offenen Zugangs (Open Access-Paradigma) gefördert werden. Wir definieren den offenen Zugang oder den ‚Open Access' als eine umfassende Quelle menschlichen Wissens und kulturellen Erbes, die von der Wissenschaftsgemeinschaft bestätigt wurden." Mit der zunehmenden Verbreitung von Open Access entstanden in Österreich u. a. institutionelle Open Access Policies von Universitäten, das nationale Netzwerk OANA (Open Science Network Austria) und das interuniversitäre Projekt „e-Infrastructures Austria"[3] (initiiert 2014) zum koordinierten Aufbau von universitären Repositorien und Netzwerkstrukturen. Dieses Potenzial galt es für das Projekt „Open Education Austria" (mit Start Mitte 2016) zu nutzen und weiter zu entfalten.

Internationale Projektvorhaben wie CORE-Materials in Großbritannien[4], OpenEd@UCL in Großbritannien[5], CEDEC in Spanien[6], die Bestrebungen zum Auf-

---

[2] Siehe https://openaccess.mpg.de/68053/Berliner_Erklaerung_dt_Version_07-2006.pdf

[3] Siehe https://e-infrastructures.univie.ac.at

[4] Siehe http://www.core.materials.ac.uk CORE-Materials: Collaborative Open Resource Environments for Materials

bau von OER-Repositorien an deutschen Hochschulen oder auch offene Angebote wie MOOCs haben dazu inspiriert, ein österreichweites Netzwerk bzw. Portal zu etablieren.

Offene Bildungsressourcen aus dem Hochschulbereich sind aus mehrerlei Gründen schwer auffindbar. Universitätslehrende erarbeiten sich im Rahmen ihrer Lehrtätigkeit eigenständig und meist als Einzelkämpfer/innen ihre eigenen, fachlich hochwertigen Lehr-/Lernmaterialien und stellen diese einem eingegrenzten Benutzerkreis (in den meisten Fällen im Rahmen einer Lehrveranstaltung) zur Verfügung. Universitäre Fach-Communities sind zwar vernetzt, doch die Verbreitung von Lehr/Lernmaterialien im Sinne einer Qualitätssteigerung spielt bisher keine allzu große Rolle. Mit dem Projekt „Open Education Austria" sollte für Lehrende die Möglichkeit eröffnet werden, „Openness" im Sinn eines Wissenstransfers in die breite Öffentlichkeit zu praktizieren.

Zeitgleich zum Projekt wurden „Empfehlungen für die Integration von Open Educational Resources an Hochschulen in Österreich" erarbeitet. Die Arbeitsgruppe „Open Educational Resources" des Forum neue Medien in der Lehre Austria (fnm-austria)[7] konnte den Weg für eine breite Sensibilisierung von Lehrenden und Hochschulen bezüglich OER aufbereiten und zur Akzeptanz dieser Praxis beitragen.

---

[5] Siehe http://open-education-repository.ucl.ac.uk Ein institutionelles Repository zum Uploaden, Veröffentlichen, Archivieren und Teilen von OER des University College London.

[6] Siehe http://cedec.intef.es/recursos/ Centro Nacional de Desarrollo Curricular en Sistemas no Propietarios.

[7] Siehe http://fnm-austria.at/fileadmin/user_upload/documents/Buecher/2016_fnma-OER-Empfehlungen_final.pdf

3 Services zur OER-Entwicklung

Im Projekt werden Lehrende dabei unterstützt, sowohl bestehende digitale Lehr-/Lernmaterialien in Kooperation mit inner- und interuniversitären Fachkolleginnen/-kollegen mediendidaktisch weiterzuentwickeln als auch neue digitale Lehr-/Lernmaterialien (z. B. in Form von Videos, interaktiven Skripten, Online-Kursen, Grafiken, Podcasts) für ihre Lehre zu entwickeln und als OER qualitätsgesichert zu veröffentlichen.

Unter OER werden hier digitale Lehr-/Lernmaterialien verstanden, die unter Creative-Commons-Lizenzen veröffentlicht sind und damit über das geltende Urheberrecht hinaus das Weiterverwenden und Wiederveröffentlichen in einer nächsten Version ermöglichen.

Im Projekt ist „Openness" als Überbegriff für ein flexibles, anpassungsfähiges Grundprinzip angelegt (vgl. BAKER, 2017).

In der Kommunikation mit Lehrenden wurden als Argumente für OER hervorgehoben:

Offene Bildungsressourcen

- stärken die geforderte „Openness" von universitärer Lehre (Lebenslanges Lernen, „Third Mission" der Universitäten zur Anbindung an die Gesellschaft);
- lösen eine schrittweise Qualitätssteigerung des Lehrens und Lernens aus und steigern die Reputation des Standorts;
- tragen dazu bei, dass Lehrende Wertschätzung innerhalb der Fachgemeinschaft erfahren, die Qualität ihrer Lehre sichtbar wird und Lehrmaterialien zitierbar sind;
- ermöglichen es Studienwerberinnen/-werbern, sich effizient auf Aufnahmeverfahren bzw. Studien vorzubereiten;
- erleichtern besonders Studienbeginnerinnen/-beginnern selbstständigen Wissenserwerb und das Verstehen komplexer Inhalte.

Die niederschwellige Unterstützung der Contenterstellung nimmt einen hohen Stellenwert ein, um Lehrende für die Praxis der freien Zugänglichkeit ihrer Materialien zu gewinnen. Die von der Universität Wien und Universität Innsbruck angebotenen Services zur OER-Erstellung und OER-Veröffentlichung stoßen an herausfordernde infrastrukturelle wie auch urheberrechtliche Aspekte.

In der universitären Diskussion wird OER zunehmend mit OEP (Open Educational Practices) kontextualisiert, insbes. im Sinn von Teilen guter Praxis (z. B. didaktische Modellen), Zugänglichkeit universitärer Inhalte für die breite Öffentlichkeit (Third Mission) und damit Ermöglichung von informellen Lernen (vgl. BOZKURT, KOSEOGLU & SINGH, 2019). An der Universität Wien unterstützen eigens qualifizierte E-Producer/innen (meist studentische Mitarbeiter/innen) die Lehrenden bei der mediendidaktischen und technischen Gestaltung der OER. Expertinnen/Experten der Universitätsbibliothek werden bei Bedarf herangezogen und stehen für Lehrende bei offenen Fragen zur Verfügung. Die Sensibilisierung der Lehrenden für Open-Source-Produkte, OER und offene Lernformate wird durch universitätsinterne Veranstaltungen (thematische Workshops, Open House, Information der Funktionsträger/innen im Bereich Lehre sowie aller Lehrenden über den „Newsletter Lehre" des Rektorats) in Gang gesetzt, sodass Lehrende mittlerweile aktiv auf das Service-Team zukommen. Das Angebot der E-Producer/innen wird sehr gut in Anspruch genommen und beinhaltet auch Anschubhilfestellungen, Beratungen sowie informelle Workshops, um zur Selbsthilfe zu befähigen.

Eine vorläufige Gesamtdarstellung aller im Rahmen des Projektes geschaffener offener Bildungsressourcen findet sich hier.

Neben der Materialentwicklung werden Lehrende dahingehend unterstützt, ihre OER nach dem Ownerprinzip zu veröffentlichen. Ziel ist es, dass Lehrende als Urheber/innen auf Basis von Beratungsmaterial sowie Qualifizierung (siehe unten, Kap. 5) informiert entscheiden, unter welcher Creative-Commons-Lizenz sie ihre Werke veröffentlichen wollen. Hier war und ist es essenziell, individuelle Lizenzberatungen für individuellen Content anzubieten und keine standardisierten Creative-Commons-Lizenzempfehlungen für OER zu geben. Die Wünsche der Lehrenden als Urheber/innen hinsichtlich Nachnutzung, Einsatzgebiete und Formate im Rahmen der Creative-Commons-Lizenzbedingungen werden soweit wie möglich gemeinsam umgesetzt.

Die Bereitstellung der OER erfolgt in den meisten Anwendungsfällen via Lernmanagementsystem – zur besseren Sichtbarkeit wird zudem die Archivierung der OER im universitätseigenen Repositorium Phaidra empfohlen, um die Anbindung an das Fachportal und damit die Sichtbarkeit und Nachnutzung der Materialien zu gewährleisten.

4   Das OEA-Fachportal

Neben der zentral bereitgestellten physischen Infrastruktur für Lehrende (Medienlabor, Aufnahmeraum u. Ä.) sind eine OER-Clearingstelle (Bündelung mediendidaktischer, bibliothekarischer, urheberrechtlicher, technischer Services) sowie das Fachportal (verfügbar ab Juni 2019 auf openeducation.at) in Planung bzw. Umsetzung. Die technische Infrastruktur für das Portal basiert auf den Vorarbeiten des Projektes „e-Infrastructures Austria", in dem Repositorien an den Universitäten aufgebaut wurden. In den lokalen Repositorien werden die OER archiviert, versioniert und lizenziert abgelegt. Alle Objekte werden der Ownerin/dem Owner eindeutig zugeordnet und können vom dieser/diesem im jeweiligen Zugang weltöffentlich oder für einen beschränkten Nutzerkreis zugänglich gemacht werden. Das Portal, das bereits als Pilot vorliegt, greift die Information öffentlicher Objekt ab und stellt sie an einen zentralen Ort zur Nachnutzung zur Verfügung, sodass interuniversitäre Kooperationen zwischen Fachkolleginnen/-kollegen ermöglicht werden. Der Import aus universitätsinternen Archivsystemen ist bereits in Einzelfällen umgesetzt, andere und zukünftige Partneruniversitäten benötigen für die Anbindung ein kompatibles Archivsystem (siehe Ziele im parallelen Hochschulraum-Strukturmittel Projekt „e-Infrastructures Austria Plus" 2017-2019).

Bei der Konzeption des Fachportals wurden auch Anregungen aus dem Beitrag „Aufbau und Vernetzung eines Repositoriums" (MÜLLER & SCHOLZ, 2012) aufgegriffen. Der Beitrag verweist u. a. auf die Deutsche Initiative für Netzwerkinformation (DINI)[8] und gibt Hinweise für Qualitätskriterien und Erfolgsfaktoren von Open-Access-Repositorien, an denen sich wissenschaftliche Fachportale orientieren können:

- **Bündelung** der Repositorien und Kollektionen, um inhaltliche Beliebigkeit zu vermeiden und qualitative Mindeststandards zu gewährleisten.
- **Vertrauenswürdigkeit bei der Zielgruppe**, wenngleich Repositorien i. d. R. keine Begutachtungssysteme wie Online-Fachzeitschriften vorsehen. Das DINI-Zertifikat für Dokumente- und Publikationsservices 2010 bietet auch einen Kriterienkatalog, der u. a. Sichtbarkeit des Gesamtangebots, Unterstützung der Autorinnen/Autoren, rechtliche Aspekte, Informationssicherheit, Erschließung und Langzeitarchivierung umfasst.
- **Vernetzung und Einbettung**: Das Repositorium übernimmt idealerweise die Funktion eines „Schaufensters" der Einrichtung bzw. Fachgemeinschaft.
- **Zentraler Erfolgsindikator** ist die Akzeptanz eines Repositoriums bei der Fachgemeinschaft, Erfolg bemisst sich an der Nutzung durch die jeweilige Zielgruppe.

Weitere Qualitätskriterien bietet die Diskussion zu Repositorien für Open Educational Resources (vgl. Qualitätsindikatoren nach ATENAS & HAVEMANN, 2014). Bis zum Projektabschluss werden die Qualitätskriterien für das Fachportal im Konsortium abgestimmt und sollen in der Folge handlungsleitend wirken.

Vor diesem Hintergrund bietet das OEA-Fachportal:

---

[8] http://www.dini.de/dini-zertifikat/liste-der-repositorien/

- **Weltweiten Zugang** für die archivierten OER. Das Portal ist für Suchmaschinen optimiert, die OERs können daher z. B. über Google gefunden werden.
- **Facettensuche**: Damit wird es den Benutzerinnen/Benutzern des Portals ermöglicht, die Suchergebnisse nach Merkmalen einzuschränken, um bessere Suchergebnisse zu erzielen.
- **Allgemein gültige Metadaten-Standards** für OER, wie z. B. LOM – Learning Object Model LOM-Schema sowie ein Klassifikationssystem der Statistik Austria (ÖFOS) für den Austausch der Informationen zwischen den unterschiedlichen universitären Systemen.
- **Definierten Workflow** für die Übergabe von Daten aus einem Lernmanagementsystem in ein Repository.
- **Schnittstelle** zwischen dem Lernmanagementsystem Moodle und dem lokalen Repository der TU Graz[9] (diese Schnittstelle soll für weitere Moodle-Installationen nutzbar gemacht werden).

Derzeit bietet das Fachportal für Lehrende der Universität Wien folgendes Interface:

---

[9] Es wurde dazu an der TU Graz ein Plug-in für das LMS (Learning Management System) Moodle entwickelt, mit dem Materialien von Moodle in das lokale Repository der Universitätsbibliothek exportiert werden können und mit einer entsprechend offenen Lizenz versehen werden. Nur qualifizierte OER-Lehrende erhalten die Möglichkeit, dieses Plug-in zu nutzen.

Abb. 2: Screenshot Pilot Fachportal

Die folgende Grafik zeigt das architektonische Konzept des Portals. Leitmotiv war die einfache Anbindung unterschiedlicher Quellen, daher wird nicht nur über Standardschnittstellen wie OAI-PMH geharvestet, sondern es können auch Connectoren für beliebige Quellen verwendet werden. Ein weiterer Ausbau für Maschine Learning ist angedacht.

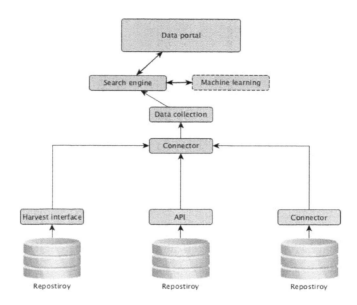

Abb. 2: Architektur Fachportal, GANGULY, 2018

5   Die OER-Qualifizierung

Neben den institutionellen Rahmenbedingungen (Policies, Strategien) und technische Infrastrukturen ist die Sensibilisierung der Lehrenden maßgeblich für die Akzeptanz von OER (vgl. GRÖBLINGER, KOPP & ZIMMERMANN, 2018). Es wurde ein Qualifizierungsprogramm der Universität Graz durchgeführt, bestehend aus den drei Teilen „Präsenz-Workshop" (an den im Projekt beteiligten Universitäten), MOOC „COER17" und „COER18" und der Abschlussveranstaltung „OER-Festival". Die Qualifizierung wurde erstmalig im Mai 2017 mit der Vergabe von OER-Zertifikaten abgeschlossen (siehe https://openeducation.at/aktivitaeten/). Neben einem formellen Qualifizierungsangebot wird den Lehrenden auch ein komprimierter OER-Leitfaden auf Deutsch und Englisch zur Verfügung gestellt.

6 Lessons learned

Durch das Projekt und dessen Umfeld konnte die Akzeptanz der Lehrenden für OER erhöht werden. Rückblickend können als Erfolgsfaktoren identifiziert werden:

- Im Projekt stehen die **Lehrenden im Mittelpunkt**. Als Fachexpertinnen/-experten und Urheber/innen erhalten sie niederschwellige Unterstützung bei der Erstellung, Archivierung, Veröffentlichung ihrer Materialien.

- Das Service-, Beratungs- und Qualifizierungsangebot erleichtert die Entwicklung und kohärente Einbettung der Materialien in unterschiedliche Lehr-/Lernkontexte, aber auch informierte urheberrechtliche (Lizenz-)Entscheidungen. Als Argumente für OER wurden v. a. Sichtbarkeit, Reputationsgewinn, Auffindbarkeit und das Potenzial der Nachnutzung herangezogen. Zur Akzeptanz hat auch beigetragen, dass OER verknüpft mit den parallelen Initiativen „Flipped Classroom in Großlehrveranstaltungen" sowie frei zugängliche „Lernmaterialien für Aufnahmeverfahren" eingeführt wurden.

- Für das Hochschulraum-Strukturmittel-Projekt war es auch erforderlich, dass das Rektorat das Vorhaben von Beginn an mitträgt und die Ziele an **Funktionsträger/innen im Bereich Lehre** und Lehrende kommuniziert.

- Die beteiligten **Dienstleistungseinrichtungen** erhalten mit dem Projekt einen übergreifenden Rahmen, um für OER-Services und Infrastrukturen Knowhow gemeinsam aufzubauen und ergebnisorientiert zu kooperieren.

- Das **nationale Umfeld** (Netzwerke wie OANA zur Open Access und fnm-austria zu OER, universitäre Policies für Open Access, das Hochschulraum-Strukturmittel-Projekt „e-Infrastructures Austria/Plus") begünstigt OER.

Zu Projektabschluss zeigen sich als zentrale Nachhaltigkeitsaspekte:

- Zwar wurde das Angebot zur Erstellung, Archivierung, freien Lizenzierung bisher gut angenommen, offen jedoch ist die Frage der universitätsübergreifenden **Nachnutzung der Materialien** durch andere Lehrende ab Veröffentlichung des Fachportals im Juni 2019.

- Die **Verstetigung der Services für Lehrende** (möglichst alle Aspekte zu OER im Sinn einer Clearingstelle gebündelt) ist mit Ressourcen verbunden und stellt eine Herausforderung dar.

- Das breite **Ausrollen des Fachportals** über den Pilot hinaus unter Berücksichtigung von Qualitätskriterien ist ebenfalls ressourcenabhängig.

- Verstetigung und Ausrollen erfordern interne Entwicklungen der beteiligten Universitäten (stabile Kooperationen zwischen den Dienstleistungseinrichtungen, teilweise auch Aufbau von institutionellen Repositorien) sowie **interuniversitäre Vernetzung** und Abstimmungen (v. a. bezüglich Fachportal). Für Letzteres gilt es mit Projektende 2019 einen Rahmen zu schaffen.

- In Zukunft soll auch ein stärkerer Fokus auf die Qualität der bereitgestellten OER gelegt werden, indem die Schnittstellen zu parallelen Initiativen gestärkt werden (insbes. zur geplanten nationalen OER-Zertifizierungsstelle[10] für Hochschulen des Vereins FNMA).

- Ebenso gilt es künftig eine Perspektivenerweiterung von OER hin zu Openness im breiteren Sinn (Open Educational Practices, Open Science) zu stärken sowie die Vernetzung mit vergleichbaren europäischen Initiativen.

---

[10] https://www.fnm-austria.at/fileadmin/user_upload/documents/Buecher/OER_Labeling_2017.pdf

Werkstattbericht

7 Literaturverzeichnis

Arbeitsgruppe „Nationale Strategie" des Open Access Network Austria (OANA) (2015). *Empfehlungen für die Umsetzung von Open Access in Österreich.* https://ojs.univie.ac.at/index.php/voebm/article/view/1299, Stand vom 20. Februar 2019.

Arbeitsgruppe „Open Educational Resources" des Forum neue Medien in der Lehre Austria (fnm-austria) (2016). *Empfehlungen für die Integration von Open Educational Resources an Hochschulen in Österreich.* https://www.fnm-austria.at/fileadmin/user_upload/documents/Buecher/2016_fnma-OER-Empfehlungen_final.pdf, Stand vom 20. Februar 2019.

Atenas, J. & Havemann, L. (2014). Questions of quality in repositories of open educational resources: a literature review. *Research in Learning Technology, 22.* https://doi.org/10.3402/rlt.v22.20889

Baker, F. W. (2017). An alternative approach: Openness in education over the last 100 years. *TechTrends, 61*(2), 130-140. https://doi.org/10.1007/s11528-016-0095-7

Bozkurz, A., Koseoglu, S. & Singh, L. (2019). An analysis of peet reviewed publications on openness in education in half a century: Trends and patterns in the open hemisphere. *Australasian Journal of Educational Technology, 35*(4), 78-97. https://doi.org/10.14742/ajet.4252

Deutsche UNESCO-Kommission (2007). *Open Access. Chancen und Herausforderungen – ein Handbuch.* https://www.unesco.de/sites/default/files/2018-06/Open_Access_0.pdf, Stand vom 20. Februar 2019.

Deutsche UNESCO-Kommission (2012). *Pariser Erklärung zu OER.* https://www.unesco.de/sites/default/files/2018-05/Pariser%20Erkl%C3%A4rung_DUK%20%C3%9Cbersetzung.pdf, Stand vom 20. Februar 2019.

Heinen, R. et al. (2016). A Federated Reference Structure for Open Informational Ecosystems. *Journal of Interactive Media in Education*, 2016(1), 13, 1-6. https://doi.org/10.5334/jime.413

Müller, U. & Scholze, F. (2012). Aufbau und Vernetzung eines Repositoriums. In Arbeitsgruppe Open Access der Schwerpunktinitiative Digitale Information der Allianz der deutschen Wissenschaftsorganisationen (Hrsg.), *Open-Access-Strategien für wissenschaftliche Einrichtungen. Bausteine und Beispiele* (S. 13-15). http://gfzpublic.gfz-potsdam.de/pubman/item/escidoc:478911/component/escidoc:478910/allianzoa_strategien_005.pdf, Stand vom 20. Februar 2019.

Open Access. Max-Planck-Gesellschaft (2006). *Berliner Erklärung über den offenen Zugang zu wissenschaftlichem Wissen.* https://openaccess.mpg.de/68053/Berliner_Erklaerung_dt_Version_07-2006.pdf, Stand vom 20. Februar 2019.

UNESCO (2015). *Open Educational Resources (OER).* https://en.unesco.org/themes/building-knowledge-societies/oer, Stand vom 20. Februar 2019.

Wiley, D. et al. (2014). Open Educational Resources: A Review of the Literature. In J. Spector, M. Merrill, J. Elen & M. Bishop (Hrsg.), *Handbook of Research on Educational Communications and Technology* (S. 781-789). New York: Springer. https://link.springer.com/chapter/10.1007/978-1-4614-3185-5_63, Stand vom 20. Februar 2019.

Autorinnen/Autoren

Mag. Dr. Sylvia LINGO ‖ Universität Wien, Center for Teaching and Learning ‖ Universitätsstr. 5 / 3. Stock, A-1010 Wien

https://ctl.univie.ac.at

sylvia.lingo@univie.ac.at

Dr. Paolo BUDRONI ‖ Universität Wien, Universitätsbibliothek ‖ Universitätsring 1, A-1010 Wien

paolo.budroni@univie.ac.at

Dipl.-Ing. (FH) Raman GANGULY ‖ Universität Wien, Zentraler Informatikdienst ‖ Universitätsstraße 7, A-1010 Wien

https://zid.univie.ac.at

raman.ganguly@univie.ac.at

Mag. Dr. Charlotte ZWIAUER ‖ Universität Wien, Center for Teaching and Learning ‖ Universitätsstr. 5 / 3. Stock, A-1010 Wien

https://ctl.univie.ac.at

charlotte.zwiauer@univie.ac.at

Thomas BAUMGARTNER[1] (Innsbruck)

Innovation through distance: The foundation of a satellite campus and its implication on teaching activities in a STEM subject

Abstract

This article discusses a technology-driven innovation in distance education at Universität Innsbruck that was commenced in 2016/17, when the already established undergraduate programme of Mechatronics was also introduced at a new satellite campus 200 kilometres away from the main campus. It looks at changing practices in teaching for this study progamme and articulates general managerial recommendations for introducing such large-scale changes. The analysis is supported by three interviews with leading faculty members and an ICT expert from Universität Innsbruck.

Keywords

Distance education, satellite campus, innovation, faculty member perpection, ICT tools

---

[1] email: thomas.baumgartner@uibk.ac.at

Scientific Contribution · DOI: 10.3217/zfhe-14-02/04

1 Introduction

The object of investigation is a technology-driven innovation in teaching at Universität Innsbruck that was commenced in the study year 2016/17, when the already established undergraduate programme of Mechatronics, offered by the Faculty of Engineering Sciences, was also introduced at a new satellite campus in Lienz, a town approximately 200 kilometres away from the main campus in Innsbruck. This could only be realized through major investments in ICT infrastructure, personnel and adjustments to the didactics of several lectures, which were then live streamed from Innsbruck to Lienz. To a great extent the project was stimulated by the regional government of Tyrol, who offered additional funding for the setup of the new undergraduate programme in Lienz as part of their regional development strategy (UNIVERSITÄT INNSBRUCK, 2015a). I will explain this in more detail in the following chapter and give additional background information on the broader context.

To group the key issues for managing this change I will use (and partly re-group) SOMEKH's stages of innovation (2007) to structure the discussion of this innovation process as follows:

- Orientation and preparation
- Routine implementation
- Refinement and (creative) integration

The model was chosen as a conceptual orientation to describe and analyze the given innovation, as it broadly covers the central stages of ICT-related innovation processes. Within the different stages it will be helpful to analyse the given example through the lens of sociocultural theory, which puts an emphasis on the change of social practices as the key indicator for enhancement taking place. I will do this by examining the undergraduate programme in Lienz as an 'activity system' with different elements and connections between them, as laid out in TROWLER, SAUNDERS & BAMBER (2009). I will put a particular focus on the tools facilitating this change, how they are used by faculty members, and if practices have changed throughout the innovation process. This transformation-centred approach takes into account the multi-level complexity of change in higher education and the importance of changing practices.

I will support my analysis by three semi-structured interviews that I have conducted with central change agents that were and are involved in this innovation process: Rudolf Stark, then Dean of Studies of the Faculty when the undergraduate programme in Lienz was introduced in 2016; Hans-Peter Schröcker, Dean of Studies from March 2017 onwards and former coordinator for new media within the Faculty; and Ortrun Gröblinger, head of the division for new media, a central administrative unit of Universität Innsbruck that offers support for ICT-related teaching matters. Furthermore, I was personally involved in this teaching innovation as well, as I administered the funding from the regional government on behalf of the Rector and acted as the interface between the Faculty and the Rector on all budgetary as well as managerial issues.

The chosen approach offers an analytical framework to map how change is taking place throughout different stages of an innovation process. As such, it offers a structured way to cluster and discuss the presented case study, and, building on this analytical part, articulate managerial responses and recommendations. Designed fit-for-purpose, the model might not be applicable in other settings, but could be a valuable source for follow-up case studies in other environments.

In my conclusion, I will summarise the key issues for managing the implemented and still ongoing teaching innovation and discuss to what extent practices have changed. I will argue that, although the change has originally been mainly resource and top-down driven, has constantly gained acceptance among faculty members involved and is more and more perceived as an opportunity to enhance didactics and thus the learning experience of students.

2 Background: Establishing a satellite campus on the periphery of Tyrol

Regarding third-party funding, which is of increasing importance for the overwhelmingly federally funded Austrian universities, the regional government of Tyrol plays an important role for Universität Innsbruck, as it has continuously increased its budget for tertiary education activities. Between 2008 and 2016, the budget had risen by almost 70% from 19 to 32 million per year (APA – AUSTRIA PRESSEAGENTUR, 2014) and continues to grow.

One of the most important milestones in this regard was a decision of the regional government in 2012 to fund two professorships in the field of Mechatronics to strengthen regional STEM activities, which eventually led to the introduction of a new Bachelor and Master's programme in Mechatronics at Innsbruck University and also the progression of the former Faculty of Civil Engineering to a Faculty of Engineering Sciences (UNIVERSITÄT INNSBRUCK, 2012)[2].

After the successful introduction of both programmes at the main campus in Innsbruck, the regional government approached the Rectorate of Universität Innsbruck again in late 2014 with the idea to offer the Bachelor programme of Mechatronics not only in Innsbruck, but also in Lienz in Osttirol, the capital of a Tyrolean region which is confronted with a constant outflow of people ("Immer weniger Einwohner in Osttirol", 2015) and is also geographically detached from the main northern part of Tyrol.

---

[2] The programme is jointly conducted with "UMIT – Private University for Health Sciences, Medical Informatics and Technology GmbH" (UNIVERSITÄT INNSBRUCK, 2017a).

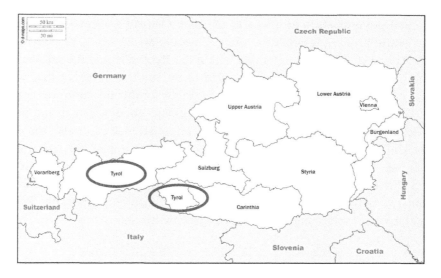

Fig. 1: Map of Austria and location of Tyrol (D-Maps.com, 2019a).

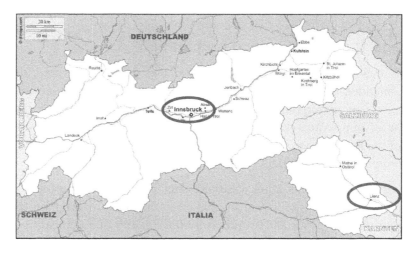

Fig. 2: Map of Tyrol and location of Lienz (D-Maps.com, 2019b).

The regional government's aim was to enhance Osttirol's attractiveness and also limit the outflow of – particularly young – people with such a new tertiary programme. After extensive consultations within the Rectorate and the affected Faculty of Engineering Sciences, it was decided to pursue the initiative that was proposed by the regional government. The main driver for this decision was for a large part the very active role and interest of the regional government in the prior and further development of the Faculty for Engineering Sciences, but also the opportunities for Universität Innsbruck in widening its regional impact through a new satellite campus and investing in academic personnel and infrastructure in an important STEM subject (UNIVERSITÄT INNSBRUCK, 2015b). How this change was managed will be discussed in the following chapters, especially how ICT-infrastructure was used to cope with the geographic distance.

3 Case study Lienz: Managing a technology-enhanced innovation in distance education

3.1 Stage 1: Orientation and preparation

According to SOMEKH (2007), this stage includes the phases where information about the intended innovation is gathered and preparations are made. In regards to setting up the new undergraduate programme in Lienz, I am therefore discussing a time frame of approximately one and a half years between late 2014, when the decision of the Rectorate to engage in this activity was taken, and the actual start of the programme in autumn 2016.

The early phase of this innovation was dominated by the question of how Universität Innsbruck deals with the logistical challenges in terms of teaching that such a new satellite campus poses. As proposed by the Faculty of Engineering Sciences, the principal decision was made very early on, that no new curriculum should be introduced. Instead, all courses from the existing programme in Innsbruck should also be offered in Lienz. This was critical insofar as the curriculum of the Mechatronics programme is highly interdisciplinary and large parts of the programme are made up of basic lectures like mathematics, electronics, physics or chemistry that are taught by very senior academics and also attended by students of other undergraduate programmes offered by the Faculty (UNIVERSITÄT INNSBRUCK, 2017b). Thus they could not simply be duplicated in Lienz. Both the Rectorate and the Faculty saw the use of ICT-tools and E-Learning as a possibility to cope with this challenge, by live streaming all basic lectures from Innsbruck to Lienz, while offering all other interactive courses (like laboratories) on the ground in Lienz. Therefore, E-Learning at this early stage intentionally only encompassed live streaming as an additional means to deliver teaching – a conception that considers ICT-tools as neutral and largely ignores their impact on teachers and their ways of teaching, which several academics critique, such as KIRKWOOD & PRICE (2014), KNOX (2013), and BAYNE (2015).

Because of this misconception and the manifold notions of e-learning, rather intense discussions and also resistance arose within the Faculty, particularly among the affected faculty members. It was the then Dean of Studies Rudolf Stark, supported by the division for new media headed by Ms Gröblinger, who coordinated and led the discussion within the Faculty to elicit compromises and ensure support. This was successful and looked as follows: Established teaching routines need to change as little as possible, however, the sole use of live streaming was seen as insufficient (R. Stark, personal communication, November 17, 2017). It was widely agreed that students in Lienz should not only be able to listen passively to lectures happening in Innsbruck, but also interact with teachers in a bi-directional way, e.g. for questions or discussions. Consequently, the ICT-infrastructure, as originally foreseen, needed to be extended by hardware and software for videoconferencing to meet the demands made by faculty members involved. Furthermore, additional student support staff were requested to assist academics involved in the new project. Confronted with these requirements, which also had substantial budgetary consequences that were originally not foreseen, the Rector agreed to cover these additional costs in order not to endanger the project as a whole.

From these considerations and contrasted with relevant literature, several key issues can be derived that support managing change in the early phase of a teaching
innovation of such a scale:

- **Clear aim:** It was a shared understanding both from the Rectorate as well
  as the Faculty that the undergraduate programme in Lienz should be established by autumn 2016. Without this message, which was clearly top-
  down, and the corresponding time pressure, discussions within the Faculty
  would probably have been more complicated and inertia greater. However,
  as TROWLER, MURRAY & KNIGHT (2003, p. 3) point out, *'pervasive
  change takes time'* and needs long-term thinking.

- **Adaptiveness 1:** While the aim was clear, the original intention to exclu-
  sively use live streaming needed to be adapted in accordance with the requirements of faculty members involved. Here managing change in a higher education institution differs from change in the corporate world insofar
  as a more inclusive approach is needed that is in line with academic values
  (D'ANDREA & GOSLING, 2005). Hence change agents within higher
  education need to be flexible when managing change – in particular to
  structures and scope of change – and also allow devolved responsibilities,
  facilitating solutions that are fit for purpose.

- **Creating ownership:** In the case of a large scale teaching innovation like
  Lienz, that not only combined the establishment of a new satellite campus,
  but also the introduction of e-learning elements in an existing curriculum,
  much of the success is dependent on the faculty members involved in the
  programme. SALMON (2005) highlights that for e-learning innovations in
  higher education institutions, ownership for content and pedagogy must lie
  within the respective academic departments to ensure wide support among
  academics. In the case of Lienz, this was ensured through the deliberations
  conducted by the then Dean of Studies Rudolf Stark, who was a long-time
  and respected member of the Faculty. The propositions made by this group
  were translated into the technical and personnel (student support staff) ne-

cessities, therefore creating ownership for the setup that was ultimately realized.

Another important aspect that Hans-Peter Schröcker (personal communication, November 14, 2017), who was also involved in these initial discussions, pointed out, is the aspect that the freedom to not change teaching practices at all was a prerequisite for faculty members to engage in this project. This absence of pressure to align with any guidelines of ICT-supported didactics allowed faculty members to retain autonomy over their courses and pedagogy – which does not mean that change is not ultimately happening.

- **Resources and institutional strategy:** While TROWLER et al. (2003) softens the importance of sufficient financial resources when delivering change, additional investments in ICT-infrastructure and support staff were a prerequisite to make progress. These additional funds were provided by the Rector due to the overall strategic importance of Lienz as outlined in the background chapter. All interviewees highlighted the importance of adequate funding for the successful initial implementation of the project, leading ultimately to the adaption of six lecture halls with state of the art ICT-infrastructure for the chosen setup.

3.2 Stage 2: Routine implementation

For SOMEKH (2007) routine implementation in ICT-related innovations takes place when low-level, routine use is established by those involved. Applied to Lienz this was the case for the first study year beginning in October 2016, when the new satellite campus officially opened and former Innsbruck-only based lectures of the Bachelor programme of Mechatronics were transmitted to Lienz through live streaming and video conferencing.

The problems arising from the very tool-limited understanding of ICT can be shown by the question of how to use blackboards when live streaming lectures. They are still quite common in several subjects like mathematics or mechanics and it was a request from faculty members involved that the picture of the blackboard needs to be transmitted to the satellite campus (Gröblinger, personal communication, November 10, 2017). This poses several challenges for live streaming, particularly in regards to readability.

In her interview Gröblinger (personal communication, November 10, 2017) points out that her division proposed the use of tablets instead of blackboards to ensure readability, which was initially not very widely picked up. However, during the course of the first study year and mostly due to student responses, faculty members more and more switched to tablet use in order to provide students in Lienz with a more readable version of their written explanations delivered in class. This example shows the discrepancies arising from a top-down and technology-centred approach against the realities on the ground, when change is not driven by the intrinsic professional motivation of teachers. If ICT is considered as integral to learning, PEARSON & SOMEKH (2006) argue that tools and the learning process need to be aligned, which was originally not the case in this example.

Another example of reluctant adoption during the routine implementation phase was the resistance to recording of lectures, which was proposed by the division for new media to cope with possible technical difficulties. Intended as a means to provide students with a backup version of the lecture, recording was perceived as a threat to replace future lectures with these records. Gröblinger (personal communication, November 10, 2017) explains that there was, in general, substantial fear regarding the new ICT-tools and how to use them appropriately, requiring a large amount of individual training of academics involved. Similar views are shared by Schröcker (personal communication, November 14, 2017), who explains that an informal feedback session organized among involved faculty members in January 2017 was particularly helpful to identify room for improvement when incorporating ICT-tools into lectures. Such a format indicates that efforts to change practices and make progress have happened on the ground and professional improvement is taken very seriously by faculty members involved.

In regards to managing change in this phase of innovation, I want to highlight two important aspects that need to be considered:

- **Adaptiveness 2:** SALMON (2005) argues that there are two ways of introducing e-learning into traditional teaching: Either through centralization and provision of professional services, or by incrementally involving affected academics and allowing them to make individual contributions. The described teaching innovation was dominantly driven by the first aspect, though devolved responsibilities allowed staff to find their own speed of adapting to the new circumstances. This not only led to a different setup of ICT-infrastructure in the build up to the implementation phase ("Adaptiveness 1"), but also acknowledged and gave room to changing practices on the ground. This room to manoeuvre on the side of faculty members involved was essential for becoming comfortable with the new situation and dealing with responses from students and among peers. This supports the argument that enhancement cannot be accredited to technology alone, but instead takes place in its respective social context (BAYNE, 2015).

- **Professional support:** As stated before, provision of professional services can play an important role in realizing change. Without an already well established and highly professional division for new media at Innsbruck University, which also played an important role in choosing the appropriate ICT-infrastructure, it is hard to envisage how this teaching innovation could have taken place. In the described case faculty members expected (but also valued) to be supported appropriately (Stark 2017, personal communication, November 17, 2017), as the rationale for the project was very much institution-driven. For instance, in the first weeks of the new study year colleagues from Ms Gröblinger's department were physically present in the lecture halls to support involved faculty members in case of any technical malfunctions (Gröblinger, personal communication, November 10, 2017).

3.3   Stage 3: Refinement and (creative) integration

Refinement and integration happens when steps are taken to integrate an innovation more broadly into practices and new approaches are pursued, which is the most challenging phase in ICT-related innovations (SOMEKH, 2007). In a recent empirical study from the Higher Education Academy about current teaching developments in the UK, 'Teaching excellence in the disciplines', the authors stress that 'engineering was the most active discipline in terms of introducing and testing a wide range of innovative pedagogic approaches' (ABBAS, ABBAS, BRAYMAN, BRENNAN & GANTOGTOKH, 2016, p. 73).

Mechatronics as a strongly engineering-dominated programme would therefore offer good overall conditions for real change taking place – understood as changing practices – and Gröblinger (personal communication, November 10, 2017) emphasises that academics supported through her division were in general rather pragmatic about implementing change. For instance, more and more academics involved in the discussed teaching innovation agree to have their lectures recorded and provide them online to students for a limited time, in case any technical difficulties occur. Schröcker (personal communication, November 14, 2017) also points out that it would be useful to use the experiences from the early implementation phase of Lienz to progress toward more comprehensive and 'real' e-learning formats that could then be disseminated. However, change is still happening on a case by case basis and is not organized in a more systemic way, in order to exploit additional learning benefits (e.g. by making these records also accessible for exam preparations) or even restructure the overall didactics of the courses.

Taking account of relevant innovation literature, the following suggestions could be considered in managing change in this advanced phase of innovation:

- **Showcase best-practices:** Creative ideas and hence best-practices are an important driver for innovation (AMABILE, CONTI, COON, LAZENBY & HERRON, 1996). In regards to Lienz, Stark (2017, personal communication, November 17, 2017) highlights that, for instance, one of the lectures enhanced through ICT-tools was nominated through the Rectorate for the national 'Ars Docendi Teaching Award' and is now listed in the national encyclopaedia of good teaching practices (ATLAS DER GUTEN LEHRE, 2017).

However, it must also be taken into account that change is highly contextual and simple transfer of knowledge is likely to fail if not 'translated' between the respective environments (TROWLER et al., 2009). But, as the challenges for academics involved in the ICT-innovation Lienz are relatively similar, as are the contexts, the prerequisites for transferability would be good. A more structured exchange of best-practices could therefore fuel further changes and support the innovation process as a whole, by creating further ownership among academics and also increase peer-pressure to rethink one's own practices.

- **Institutional dissemination and embeddedness:** Institutional rhetoric and support can play an important role in change processes, as TROWLER et al. (2003) point out. While this was certainly the case for this innovation in its early stages, it has to be ensured on a more broader basis in the longer term, in particular on an institutional level: on the one hand through continued financial support for necessary ICT-infrastructure and ICT-related professional services, on the other hand by using infrastructure and lessons learned from this innovation for other institutional contexts and disciplines that want to or even need to engage more deeply with technology-enhanced teaching and learning. On the faculty level Stark (2017, personal communication, November 17, 2017) already notices that teaching staff not involved within the project are also making use of the new ICT-infrastructure.

However, Schröcker (2017, personal communication, November 14, 2017) also highlights the necessity for more legal and organizational certainty when engaging in ICT-related activities, for instance copyright issues, but particularly internal consequences like career progression or effects on the calculation of teaching loads. To address these issues, a working group headed by the Vice Rector for Student Affairs and Teaching and Student Affairs has been initiated.

- **Evaluation:** Apart from continuous student and self-evaluation, which has already contributed to changing practices, evaluation of the project as a whole and the chosen approach has to be foreseen after an appropriate period of routine implementation. Such an evaluation should also aim to establish a more profound understanding and more commonly agreed expectations among all stakeholders for the future in the sense of a 'shared language'. The latter is particularly important due to the diffuse nature inherent to ICT-related teaching innovations (BAYNE, 2015).

4 Conclusions

The use of Somekh's stages of innovation might imply that change in higher education institutions – in this case an ICT-related teaching innovation – happens in a linear way: preparation, implementation, refinement, integration – period. This simplification is of course not valid. Change in higher education institutions happens in a complex environment with different levels of decision making, stakeholders, disciplinary cultures and activity systems that are affecting each other. Even in the discussed project there are actually two strands of innovation taking place at the same time: The introduction of a new satellite campus as well as an ICT-related teaching innovation induced by this new campus. I tried to focus on the latter dimension by using aspects of sociocultural theory to identify and discuss changing practices, however, this change needs so be understood in a broader context with its own dynamics, which I laid out in the background chapter. This interwoven nature and complexity makes change in higher education institutions generally hard to steer from a managerial point of perspective. I try to illustrate this overall challenge in the following figure.

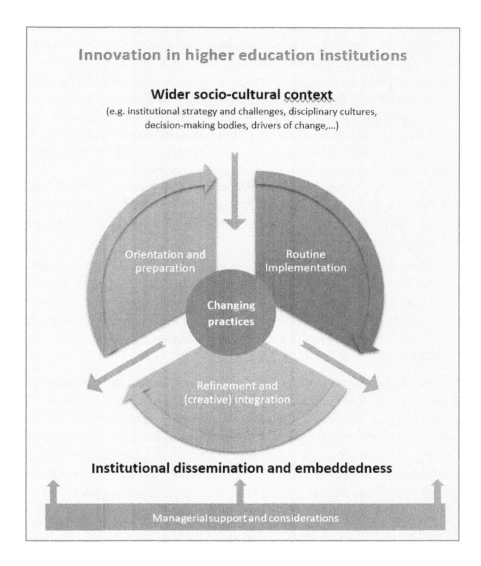

Figure 3: Adaption of Somekh's stages of innovation for illustrating change in higher education institutions

Regarding the ICT-related teaching innovation in Lienz it must be assessed that the primary driver for change was clearly top-down and resource driven. It was not the Faculty or individual faculty members who initiated a change process to enhance teaching and learning on the ground (in the sense of the diffusionist / epidemiological change theory of TROWLER et al., 2003), but the Rectorate through impetus from the regional government. Thus, ownership on the ground and willingness to change practices developed reluctantly. For such an underlying change theory TROWLER et al. (2003) point out that desired behaviour might be produced when sufficient (budgetary) allocations are provided and some bottom-up change might be evoked, however, within complex systems like universities, resistance and inertia is likely to arise if innovation is primarily pursued by one level only (SOMEKH, 2007). For the long term success of the project the following analysis seems particularly relevant:

> *Where change is imposed through managerial fiat there is unlikely to be real change in values, attitudes or practices in the long term. Real change is embedded in its context and comes when people make it their own through use and adaptation to local histories and contexts. Power and control at the ground level is a condition of success.*
> *(TROWLER et al., 2003, p. 15)*

It will therefore be crucial to align the top-down and bottom-up dimensions better, strengthen the latter and support faculty staff as much as possible to foster ownership of this project. Progress in the sense of changing practices was already made to a minor extent and some aspects of ICT-supported teaching are now embraced more widely – for instance the possibility of recording lectures. For Stark (2017, personal communication, November 17, 2017), initial scepticism towards the project has largely diminished and given way to a more curious approach of experimentation.

As the project is still in an early phase of routine implementation, an upcoming evaluation will be the appropriate occasion to change the notion of this innovation to a change process that is more driven by the professional imperative on the ground, which may also contribute more to the overall learning experience of students, as SAUNDERS et al. (2009) highlight. However, one should be cautious to potentially discourage further engagement by any centralized action plan or the like. Ultimately, this is also a concession to the inherent messiness that innovations require in order to be successful (SOMEKH, 2007) – but also makes them exciting and stimulating to be part of.

4 References

Abbas, A., Abbas, J., Brayman, K., Brennan, J., & Gantogtokh, O. (2016). *Teaching excellence in the disciplines.* Retrieved November 6, 2017, from https://www.heacademy.ac.uk/knowledge-hub/teaching-excellence-disciplines

Amabile, T. M., Conti, R., Coon, H., Lazenby, J., & Herron, M. (1996). Assessing the work environment for creativity. *Academy of Management Journal, 39*(5), 1154-1184.

APA – Austria Presse Agentur (2014, December 11). Tiroler Doppelbudget 2015/2016 – Tirol bleibt Budget-Vorzeigeland mit geringster pro-Kopf-Verschuldung (press release). Retrieved December 11, 2014, from https://www.ots.at/presseaussendung/OTS_20141211_OTS0266/tiroler-doppelbudget-20152016-tirol-bleibt-budget-vorzeigeland-mit-geringster-pro-kopf-verschuldung

Atlas der guten Lehre (2017). *Kombiniertes Face-to-Face und Distance-Learning Konzept für die Lehrveranst. „FEM–Lineare Festigkeitsanalysen" und „Festigkeitslehre in der Mechatronik" an der Universität Innsbruck mit digitaler Einbindung v. Studierenden am dislozierten Standort Lienz.* Retrieved November 17, 2017, from http://www.gutelehre.at/lehre-detail/?tx_bmwfwlehre_pi1%5Bproject%5D=520&tx_bmwfwlehre_pi1%5Bcontroller%5D=Project&tx_bmwfwlehre_pi1%5Baction%5D=detail&cHash=0252002a636a0cfb1b2818ffe5afcfbe

Bayne, S. (2015). What's the matter with 'technology-enhanced learning'? *Learning, Media and Technology, 40*(1), 5-20.

By, R. T. (2005). Organizational Change Management: A Critical Review. *Journal of Change Management, 5*(4), 369-380.

D'Andrea, V., & Gosling, D. (2005). *Improving Teaching and Learning in Higher Education: A whole institution approach*. Maidenhead: Society for Research into Higher Education.

D-maps.com (2019a, May 20). *Map Austria*. D-maps.com. Retrieved May 20, 2019, from https://d-maps.com/carte.php?num_car=4546&lang=en

D-maps.com (2019b, May 20). *Map Tyrol*. D-maps.com. Retrieved May 20, 2018, from http://d-maps.com/carte.php?num_car=34126&lang=en

Immer weniger Einwohner in Osttirol (2015, October 23). *ORF Tirol*. Retrieved November 10, 2017, from http://tirol.orf.at/news/stories/2738486/

Kirkwood, A., & Price, L. (2014). Technology-enhanced learning and teaching in higher education: what is 'enhanced' and how do we know? A critical literature review. *Learning, Media and Technology, 39*(1), 6-36.

Knox, J. (2013). The limitations of access alone: Moving towards open processes in education technology. *Open Praxis, 5*(1), 21-29.

Meriam Webster Dictionary (2017). *Innovation*. Retrieved November 9, 2017, from https://www.merriam-webster.com/dictionary/innovation

Pearson, M., & Somekh, B. (2006). Learning transformation with technology: a question of sociocultural contexts? *International Journal of Qualitative Studies in Education, 19*(4), 519-539.

Salmon, G. (2005). Flying not flapping: a strategic framework for e-learning and pedagogical innovation in higher education institutions. *Research in Learning Technology, 13*(3), 201-218.

Saunders, M., Bamber, V., & Trowler, P. (2009). Making practical sense of enhancing learning, teaching, assessment and curriculum. In V. Bamber, P. Trowler, M. Saunders, & P. Knight (Eds.), *Enhancing Learning, Teaching, Assessment and Curriculum in Higher Education: Theories, Cases and Practices* (pp. 14-20). Maidenhead: Society for Research into Higher Education & Open University Press.

Somekh, B. (2007). *Pedagogy and Learning with ICT: Researching the art of innovation.* London: Routledge.

Trowler, P., Murray, S., & Knight, P. (2003). *Change Thinking, Change Practices: a guide to change for heads of department, programme leaders and other change agents in higher education.* York: Learning and Teaching Support Network (LTSN).

Trowler, P., Saunders, M., & Bamber, V. (2009). Enhancement theories. In V. Bamber, P. Trowler, M. Saunders, & P. Knight (Eds.), *Enhancing Learning, Teaching, Assessment and Curriculum in Higher Education: Theories, Cases and Practices* (pp. 7-15). Maidenhead: Society for Research into Higher Education & Open University Press.

Universität Innsbruck (2012). *Land Tirol stiftet zwei Mechatronik-Professuren.* Retrieved November 10, 2017, from https://www.uibk.ac.at/ipoint/news/2012/land-tirol-stiftet-zwei-mechatronik-professuren.html.de

Universität Innsbruck (2015a). *Mechatronik-Studium Lienz in den Startlöchern.* Retrieved November 9, 2017, from https://www.uibk.ac.at/ipoint/blog/1358247.html

Universität Innsbruck (2015b). *Entwicklungsplan 2016-2018.* Retrieved November 11, 2017, from https://www.uibk.ac.at/universitaet/profil/dokumente/entwicklungsplan-2016-2018.pdf

Universität Innsbruck (2017a). *Bachelor's Programme Mechatronics.* Retrieved November 9, 2017, from https://www.uibk.ac.at/studium/angebot/ba-mechatronik/

Universität Innsbruck (2017b). *Curriculum for the joint Bachelor's Programme of Mechatronics of the University of Innsbruck and the UMIT – Private University for Health Sciences, Medical Informatics and Technology.* Retrieved November 11, 2017, from https://www.uibk.ac.at/fakultaeten-servicestelle/pruefungsreferate/studienplaene/english-version/ba-mechatronik_stand-01.10.2016_en.pdf

UMIT (2017). *UMIT – the health & life sciences university.* Retrieved November 10, 2017, from https://www.umit.at/page.cfm?vpath=universitaet/die-universitaet&switchLocale=en_US

Author

Dr. Thomas BAUMGARTNER ‖ Universität Innsbruck, Office of the Rector ‖ Innrain 52, 6020 Innsbruck, Austria

www.uibk.ac.at/rektorenteam/rektor/mitarbeiterinnen/

thomas.baumgartner@uibk.ac.at

Annex A – Questionnaire

Ao. Univ.-Prof. Dipl.-Ing. Dr. Rudolf Stark
(https://www.uibk.ac.at/bft/mitarbeiter/stark.html)

	German original	Translation
1	Welche Faktoren waren für die – schlussendlich erfolgreiche – Umsetzung der E-Learning Aktivitäten Lienz in der Entwicklungsphase aus deiner Sicht von besonderer Bedeutung? (bspw. Ressourcen, Einbindung der Lehrenden, etc…)	*Which factors for – the ultimately successful – implementation of e-learning activities in Lienz where particularly important during the initial development phase? (e.g. resources, involvement of academics, etc….)*
2	Wo konntest du besondere Hürden identifizieren und wie hast du versucht, damit umzugehen?	*Could you identify particular obstacles that you were confronted with and how did you deal with them?*
3	Welche Bedeutung hatten bereits bestehende best practices Beispiele – sowohl innerhalb der Fakultät als auch von außen?	*What role did established best-practices play – from within the Faculty as well as from external actors?*
4	Haben sich aus deiner Sicht Praktiken und Herangehensweisen in Bezug auf E-Learning geändert bzw. siehst du in diesem Bereich Weiterentwicklungen an der Fakultät?	*From your point of view: Have practices and approaches in regards to e-learning changed and do you see enhancement in this field within the Faculty?*
5	Im Nachhinein betrachtet: Welche Empfehlung(en) würdest du aussprechen, wenn du diese Entwicklung noch einmal begleiten würdest?	*In hindsight: Which recommendation(s) would you suggest if you would have to be part of this project again?*

assoz. Prof. Mag. Dr. Hans-Peter Schröcker
(http://geometrie.uibk.ac.at/cms/slabid-11.htm)

	German original	Translation
1	Nach dem ersten Studienjahr: Welche Faktoren sind aus deiner Sicht für die erfolgreiche Implementierung der E-Learning Aktivitäten Lienz von besonderer Bedeutung? (bspw. Ressourcen, Austausch zwischen den Lehrenden, etc…)	*After the completion of the first study year and from your point of view: Which factors for the successful implementation of e-learning activities in Lienz are of particular importance? (e.g. resources, exchange between academics, etc….)*
2	Wo kannst du noch gewissen Hürden (bzw. Berührungsängste) identifizieren?	*Can you identify particular obstacles that you are confronted with and how do you deal with them?*
3	Haben sich aus deiner Sicht Praktiken und Herangehensweisen in Bezug auf E-Learning geändert bzw. siehst du in diesem Bereich Weiterentwicklungen an der Fakultät? (etwa neue Formate des Austausches, peer learning, etc…)	*From your point of view: Have practices and approaches in regards to e-learning changed and do you see enhancement in this field within the Faculty? (e.g. new formats of exchange, peer learning, etc.)*
4	Damit verbunden: Wie geht man mit bereits gesammelten Erfahrungen um bzw. haben / hatten diese einen Einfluss auf die weiteren Planungen?	*Related to the previous question: How do you deal with lessons learned and did / do they have an impact on the further planning?*
5	Welche Empfehlung(en) würdest du für die weiteren Aktivitäten im Bereich E-Learning Lienz aussprechen?	*Which recommendation(s) would you suggest for further activities in the field of e-learning / Lienz?*

Dipl.-Ing. (FH) Ortrun Gröblinger
(https://www.uibk.ac.at/elearning/mitarbeiter/ogroeblinger.html)

	German original	Translation
1	Welche Faktoren waren aus eurer Sich für die erfolgreiche Implementierung der E-Learning Aktivitäten Lienz von besonderer Bedeutung? (bspw. Ressourcen, Beratung von Lehrenden, etc…)	*Which factors for – the ultimately successful – implementation of e-learning activities in Lienz where particularly important? (e.g. resources, consulting academics, etc….)*
2	Inwieweit ist die Fakultät bzw. sind einzelne Lehrenden an euch herangetreten, um Auskünfte / Schulungen / Input bzgl. E-Learning zu erhalten?	*To what extent did the Faculty, respectively individual academics approach you for enquiries / instruction / input in regards to e-learning?*
3	Wo konntet ihr besondere Hürden bzw. Berührungsängste identifizieren?	*Could you identify particular obstacles that you were confronted with?*
4	Haben sich aus eurer Sicht Praktiken und Herangehensweisen in Bezug auf E-Learning an der Fakultät geändert bzw. seht ihr in diesem Bereich Weiterentwicklungen an der Fakultät? (etwa neue Formate des Austausches, peer learning, etc…)	*From your point of view: Have practices and approaches in regards to e-learning changed and do you see enhancement in this field within the Faculty? (e.g. new formats of exchange, peer learning, etc.)*
5	Welche Empfehlung(en) würdet ihr für die weiteren Aktivitäten im Bereich E-Learning Lienz aussprechen?	*Which recommendation(s) would you suggest for further activities in the field of e-learning / Lienz?*

Scientific Contribution

Annex B – Streamed lectures Bachelor Mechatronics Lienz

Winter semester 2016 / 17:

844803	Precourse Descriptive Geometry	Innsbruck → Lienz
844804	Precourse Descriptive Geometry 2	Innsbruck → Lienz
844212	Mathematics 1	Innsbruck → Lienz
844138	Fundamentals of Chemistry	Innsbruck → Lienz
846122	Fundamentals of Physics	Innsbruck → Lienz
146117	Principles of Electrical Engineering	Hall (UMIT) → Lienz (4x)
844533	Mechanics in Mechatronics 1	Innsbruck → Lienz
850461	Fundamentals of Material Techno-logy 1	Innsbruck → Lienz Lienz → Innsbruck (1x)
844371	Mathematics Advanced Training Course	Innsbruck → Lienz
844502	Mechanics Advanced Training Course	Innsbruck → Lienz
846103	Physics Advanced Training Course	Innsbruck → Lienz
846302	Chemistry Advanced Training Cour-se	Innsbruck → Lienz

Summer semester 2017:

850360	Components and Basic Circuits	Hall → Lienz
844222	Mathematics 2	Innsbruck → Lienz
844861	Geometric Modelling, Visualisation and CAD in Mechatronics	Innsbruck → Lienz Lienz → Innsbruck (1x)
844122	Strength of Materials in Mechatronics	Innsbruck → Lienz
850462	Fundamentals of Material Technology 2	Innsbruck → Lienz

Sabine SEUFERT[1], Josef GUGGEMOS & Luca MOSER
(St. Gallen)

Digitale Transformation in Hochschulen: auf dem Weg zu offenen Ökosystemen

Zusammenfassung

Digitale Ökosysteme bieten in Form von offenen Lernsystemen einen neuen Gestaltungsrahmen, um die Chancen der fortgeschrittenen Digitalisierung in einer Netzwerkökonomie zu nutzen. Bildungsprozesse in einem Ökosystem ermöglichen eine individualisierte Studiengestaltung, personalisiertes Lernen auf der Basis intelligenter Systeme sowie eine stärkere Verknüpfung von Forschung und Lehre. Offene Lernökosysteme können in diesem Zusammenhang als Bindeglied zu Open Education im digitalen Bildungsraum aufgefasst werden. Das Fallbeispiel 'Digital Israel' zeigt ein derartiges Ökosystem auf der Ebene des Bildungssystems.

Schlüsselwörter

Open Educational Resoures, Ökosystem, Digitale Transformation

---

[1] E-Mail: sabine.seufert@unisg.ch

Digital transformation in higher education: Towards open ecosystems

Abstract

Digital ecosystems in the form of open learning systems offer opportunities to leverage advanced digitalisation in a network economy. Educational processes in an ecosystem allow for an individualized design of the study course, personalized learning on the basis of intelligent systems, and an increased exchange between research and teaching. In this context, open-learning ecosystems can be seen as a link to open education in the digital educational space. The 'Digital Israel' case study shows such an ecosystem at the level of the educational system.

Keywords

open educational resoures, ecosystem, digital transformation

1 Problemstellung und Zielsetzung

Die digitale Transformation verändert unsere Lebens- und Arbeitswelt derzeit fundamental (BLOSSFELD et al., 2018; OSWALD & KRCMAR, 2018). Sie gilt als eine vierte industrielle Revolution (BAUER, SCHLUND, MARRENBACH & GANSCHAR, 2014). Nach POUSTTCHI (2018) beinhaltet die digitale Transformation Veränderungen, die sich durch die Verwendung digitaler Technologien und Techniken ergeben. Dabei sind sowohl wirtschaftliche als auch gesellschaftliche Veränderungen bedeutsam. Die Transformation ist im Kontext einer Netzwerkökonomie zu verstehen. Diese wird durch eine noch stärker global vernetzte Wirtschaft angetrieben, wodurch Organisationsgrenzen verschwimmen sowie klassische Geschäftsmodelle, Arbeitsformen und -umgebungen sich verändern werden (BELLMANN, 2017).

Die digitale Transformation durchdringt alle gesellschaftlichen Bereiche mit einem je nach Bereich zwar variierenden, im Vergleich zu früheren Dekaden jedoch hohem Tempo. Ein weiterer Grund für die gesteigerte Dynamik ist die Netzwerkökonomie (ÖSTEREICH & SCHRÖDER, 2017), die durch die digitale Transformation (in Verbindung mit einer noch stärker global vernetzten Wirtschaft) angetrieben wird.

Die digitale Transformation stellt Hochschulen vor die Herausforderung, die sich bietenden Chancen zu nutzen und die Transformation mitzugestalten (GETTO, HINTZE & KERRES, 2018; SEUFERT & VEY, 2016). Dabei ist die zunehmende Digitalisierung in der Hochschullehre kein neues Phänomen. DITTLER (2017) beschreibt in einem historischen Rückblick drei Wellen des E-Learning bzw. des technologiegestützten Lehrens und Lernens an der Hochschule. Empirische Befunde in der Literatur zur Hochschulentwicklung zeigen, dass umfassende Digitalisierungsstrategien entlang der Dimensionen Organisation, Ökonomie, Kultur sowie Veränderungsprozesse und Leadership erfolgversprechend für die nachhaltige Implementation von E-Learning sind (SEUFERT, EBNER, KOPP & SCHLASS, 2015). Die kontinuierliche Weiterentwicklung der Hochschule rückte somit in den letzten Jahren stärker in den Vordergrund. Damit verbunden ist auch die Frage, wie sich Forschungsprozesse durch die Digitalisierung ändern und inwieweit sich Akteurinnen/Akteure einbinden lassen, um die Hochschule als permanentes Forschungs- und Entwicklungsprojekt zu begreifen (MORMANN & WILLJES, 2013).

Eine weitere weltweite Entwicklung im Bildungsbereich ist die Open Education Bewegung. Auch die steigende Bedeutung des Lernens in informellen Kontexten, d. h. Lernen, das im Alltag, am Arbeitsplatz, im Familienkreis oder in der Freizeit stattfindet, führt zu einer Zunahme der Bedeutung von Open Education (HOFHUES & SCHIEFNER-ROHS, 2017). Ein Diskussionsstrang im Kontext der fortschreitenden Digitalisierung bezieht sich somit darauf, welche Implikationen Open Access, Open Science sowie Open Education für Forschung und Lehre an Hochschulen haben.

Unter „Digitalisierung der Bildung" versteht KERRES (2016) „eine Kurzformel für den grundliegenden Transformationsprozess der Bildungsarbeit, der – anders als E-Learning – die gesamte Wertschöpfung der Wissenserschliessung und -kommunikation in den Blick nimmt" (S. 3). Kern der Diskussion ist dabei, dass es nicht mit einem additiven ‚Ergänzen' von Lernangeboten um soziales und mobiles Lernen getan ist, sondern dass neue Geschäftsmodelle, ein Kulturwandel und veränderte Leistungsprozesse nötig sind (DITTLER, 2017; HOFHUES & SCHIEFNER-ROHS, 2017). Wie Bildungsinstitutionen der digitalen Transformation in dieser sehr umfassenden Bedeutung über die gesamte Wertschöpfungskette hinweg begegnen können, ist bislang erst wenig erforscht (BLOSSFELD et al., 2018).

Offene Lernsysteme sind vor dem Hintergrund der digitalen Transformation umfassender zu denken als beispielsweise der Einsatz von E-Learning oder digitaler Medien in der Lehre. Wir präsentieren das Konzept eines digitalen Ökosystems und zeigen auf, wie der Entwicklungsprozess dorthin vollzogen werden kann. Das vorgestellte Konzept hat sich im Schulsystem bewährt (SEUFERT, GUGGEMOS & TARANTINI, 2018). Die Leitfrage dieses Beitrags lautet:

Wie kann der Transformationsprozess von Hochschulen hin zu einem offenen, digitalen Lernökosystem für die Hochschulbildung gestaltet werden?

In Kapitel 2 wird hierzu geklärt, mit welchen neuen Anforderungen die Hochschulbildung im Zuge der digitalen Transformation konfrontiert ist. Digitale Ökosysteme stellen dabei zentrale Rahmenbedingungen für die Hochschulbildung dar, um diesen neuen Anforderungen begegnen zu können. Auf der Basis einer Literaturanalyse schärfen wir das Verständnis von Ökosystemen im Bildungsbereich als eine Möglichkeit, mit neuen Kooperationsformen Bildungsdienstleistungen nachhaltig entwickeln zu können. Dabei beleuchten wir näher die Verbindung zur Open-Education-Bewegung, um die Besonderheiten von offenen Lernsystemen im digitalen Bildungsraum herauszuarbeiten. Aufgezeigt werden Entwicklungslinien, um Ökosysteme in der Hochschulbildung etablieren zu können. In Kapitel 3 gehen wir detailliert auf Ökosysteme als Rahmen für die Hochschulbildung ein. Anhand des Fallbeispiels ‚Digital Israel' (Makro-Ebene) zeigen wir in Kapitel 4, wie sich das Phänomen der Ökosysteme als Bildungsraum konzeptualisieren lässt und welche Potenziale es für die gemeinsame Weiterentwicklung von Bildungsangeboten bieten kann. Im abschließenden Kapitel 5 ziehen wir ein Fazit und geben einen Ausblick auf weiterführende Fragestellungen.

2 Digitale Transformation in Hochschulen: neue Anforderungen an die Hochschulbildung

Ausgehend von den dargelegten Zusammenhängen und empirischen Untersuchungen zuhanden des Staatssekretariats für Bildung, Forschung und Innovation [SBFI] (SEUFERT, 2018), verstehen wir unter digitaler Transformation im Kontext der Hochschule:

Zum einen die Organisations- bzw. Hochschulentwicklung im digitalen Wandel, der sich auf die gesamte Wertschöpfung der Wissenserschliessung und -kommunikation bezieht. Zum anderen die Befähigung der Organisationsmitglieder einer Hochschule, insbesondere Lehrende sowie Studierende, die Chancen der Digitalisierung und von Netzwerkeffekten für die Hochschulentwicklung selbständig und eigenverantwortlich zu nutzen.

Digitale Transformation in Hochschulen hat damit die ‚digitale Souveränität‘ (BLOSSFELD et. al., 2018) der Organisationsmitglieder zum Ziel, um digitale Ökosysteme und die damit verbundenen Netzwerkeffekte zu etablieren und nutzbar zu machen (SEUFERT, 2018). Der Zusammenhang zwischen dem normativen Konzept der digitalen Souveränität und der Implementierung ist in Abb. 1 dargestellt.

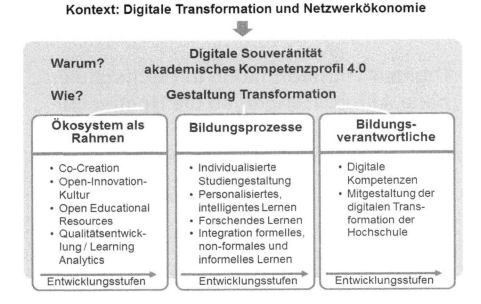

Abb. 1: Digitale Transformation in Hochschulen (eigene Abbildung)

Die geänderten Anforderungen an die Hochschulbildung können auf unterschiedlichen Ebenen betrachtet werden:

Normative Ebene: Die digitale Souveränität und ein akademisches Kompetenzprofil 4.0 als neue Ziele und Inhalte der Hochschulbildung rücken in den Vordergrund (SCHIRMERS, SCHRÖDER, SÖNMEZ & WEIHMANN, 2016). Die konkreten Forderungen sind jedoch sehr unterschiedlich. In der derzeitigen Diskussion stehen häufig fach- und berufsorientierte Kompetenzen im Vordergrund. Eine andere Extremposition fordert, dass stärker sogenannte ‚Soft Skills' zu fördern wären. Digitale Kompetenzen sind sowohl als Teil von Fachwissen und berufsorientierten Fähigkeiten als auch als Teil der Persönlichkeitsbildung zu entwickeln. Nicht ausreichend scheint, digitale Kompetenzen lediglich als ‚Hard skills' in bestehende Studiengänge zu integrieren

(BLOSSFELD et al., 2018). Eine solche Sichtweise hätte eine sehr technische und funktionale Ausrichtung zur Folge. Im Vordergrund sollte eher stehen, wie sich in einer digitalen Welt eine für den Menschen förderliche Arbeitsumgebung kreieren lässt. Führungskräfte nehmen bei der Ausgestaltung der normativen Vorgaben eine wichtige Rolle ein. Sie sollten zwar über technisches Wissen verfügen, gleichzeitig aber ein Profil weg von der technokratischen problemlösenden hin zur reflektierenden, verantwortungsvoll handelnden Persönlichkeit entwickeln (BRAHM, JENERT & EULER, 2016).

Gestaltungsebene: Ökosysteme in Form offener Lernsysteme stellen einen neuen Rahmen dar, um insbesondere Lehrende sowie auch Studierende in die Lage zu versetzen, die Chancen der fortgeschrittenen Digitalisierung in einer Netzwerkökonomie selbständig und eigenverantwortlich zu nutzen. Bildungsprozesse in einem Ökosystem ermöglichen eine individualisierte Studiengestaltung, personalisiertes Lernen auf der Basis intelligenter Systeme, eine stärkere Verknüpfung von Forschung und Lehre sowie von formalem, non-formalem und informellem Lernen. Als zentrale Erfolgsfaktoren sind nicht nur auf Seiten der Studierenden neue Kompetenzen nötig, sondern auch auf Seiten der Lehrenden: Kompetenzen zur Gestaltung von Lernmöglichkeiten in digitalen Ökosystemen sowie übergreifend zur Mitgestaltung der digitalen Transformation in der Hochschulbildung (SEUFERT, 2018).

3 Transformationsprozess der Hochschul-bildung

3.1 Ökosysteme als Rahmung der digitalen Transformation

Für Hochschulen ist es bedeutsam, für ihre vielschichtigen Aufgaben – Lehre, Forschung, Ausbildung künftiger Entscheidungsträgerinnen und Entscheidungsträger, Administration usw. – einen optimalen Umgang mit den gezeichneten Entwicklungen zu finden und sich dadurch selbst weiterzuentwickeln (GETTO, HINTZE &

KERRES, 2018). Diese komplexen Zusammenhänge erfordern neue Arbeits- und Interaktionsformen, um die Transformation angemessen zu vollziehen. Die Offenheit digitaler Plattformen ermöglicht dynamische Entwicklungen und Co-Creation-Prozesse der relevanten Akteurinnen/Akteure und den Aufbau von digitalen Ökosystemen (SEUFERT, 2018; DILLENBOURG, 2016). Digitale Ökosysteme ermöglichen durch diese Co-Creation-Prozesse sowie die interpersonale und interinstitutionelle Zusammenarbeit Netzwerkeffekte (BAHR et al., 2012). Diese helfen, die Möglichkeiten der digitalen Transformation nutzbar zu machen.

Eine Literaturanalyse zu Ökosystemen im Bildungsbereich, insbesondere der Hochschulbildung, findet sich in Tab. 1. Gemeinsam ist allen Konzepten die Partizipation und Selbstorganisation der Akteurinnen/Akteure, insbesondere auch der Lernenden, um nachhaltig ein Lernökosystem weiterzuentwickeln. Die Verbindung zu Open Education ist bislang noch wenig verbreitet. KERRES & HEINEN (2014, 2015) stellen diesen Zusammenhang explizit mit dem Konzept des ‚Informational ecosystems' im Sinne einer unabhängigen Referenzplattform her, um Open Education mit einer offen Lerninfrastruktur zu unterstützen.

Tab. 1: Ökosysteme mit Bezug zum Bildungsbereich

Referenz	Kontext	Ökosystem Konzept	Komponenten
Looi (2001)	Learning Ecosystem im Internet als Communities of Interests, basierend auf dem Prinzip der Selbstorganisation	Selbstorganisierende Communities im Netz. Mithilfe von Co-Creation-Prozessen können Designer/innen von Lernumgebungen ihre Prozesse kontinuierlich verbessern. Open Educational Resources (OER) beziehen sich insbesondere auf nutzergenerierte Inhalte.	Die Akteurinnen/Akteure teilen sich in Nischen auf, als Ort oder Rolle im Ökosystem. Je vielfältiger die Nischen, desto flexibler und fruchtbarer das Ökosystem (distribuierte Kognition). Die Interaktion der Teilnehmenden treibt die technologische und soziale Entwicklung voran.

Sedita (2003)	Knowledge Management, Dynamik des Lernprozesses auf verschiedenen Ebenen (Individuen, Organisationen, Community)	Die klassische hierarchische Beziehung zwischen Lehrpersonen und Lernenden verändert sich hin zu einer Bildung eines Knowledge Ecosystems, das über das gesamte Arbeitsleben andauern kann.	Ein Ökosystem basiert auf Wissensteilung, auf der Verbindung von formalem, non-formalem und informellem Lernen, eine Art des unstrukturierten Lernens, das auf eine große Anzahl an Akteurinnen/Akteuren einwirkt.
Dahlstrom, Brooks & Bichsel (2014)	Learning Ecosystem als eine nützliche Denkweise für die technologische Entwicklung im Hochschulkontext	Ein Learning Ecosystem ist eine komplexe Community und Umgebung, in der die Lernenden interagieren, geprägt durch eine hohe Dynamik: Zeit, Ort und Raum können sich dabei ständig verändern.	Designer/innen, Lernende und die Technologie: die Individuen sind der Organismus, physische Umgebung und IT-Infrastruktur. Die Partizipation der Beteiligten bei der Mitgestaltung des Lernökosystems ist dabei zentral (Selbstorganisation).
Galarneau (2005)	Learning Ecosystems von Massive Multiplayer Online Games	Learning Ecosystems, die auf informellem Lernen aufbauen. Social Learning in einer Umgebung, in der spontane Selbstorganisation der Teilnehmenden sehr natürlich erscheint.	Kernelement: Game. Spieler/innen engagieren sich in symbiotischen Lern-Beziehungen und unterstützen sich gegenseitig, um eine höhere Stufe im Spiel zu erlangen. Einzelpersonen interagieren auch ausserhalb des Spiels miteinander (soziale und lernende ‚Metagame'-Interaktionen).

Chang & Guetl (2007)	Learning Ecosystem, fokussiert auf E-Learning im Hochschulkontext	Learning Ecosystem mit der Fokussierung auf die Integration von E-Learning, daher auch „eLearning ecosystem" (ELES) durch die Beschränkung der Systembedingungen des vorgeschlagenen Lernökosystems auf den Bereich E-Learning.	Drei Komponenten zur Spezifikation von ELES: (A) die Besonderheiten der Lerngemeinschaften und anderer Interessengruppen, (B) die spezifischen Lernhilfen und (C) die eingeschränkten Bedingungen des Lernökosystems.
Kerres & Heinen (2014); Kerres & Heinen (2015)	Informational Ecosystems im Hochschulkontext, Verbindung zu Open Education, systematischer Umgang mit OER	Informationale Ökosysteme als eine unabhängige Referenzplattform, um Open Learning/Education mit einer offen Lerninfrastruktur zu unterstützen: - connected systems, - distributed functions, - decentralized control, - metadata exchange.	Drei Funktionalitäten: 1) Lehrperson sucht nach OER (auf einer Referenzplattform), 2) verlinkt zur Ressource und 3) stellt den Inhalt in einer Lernplattform zur Verfügung. Inhalte von verschiedenen Anbietenden, aber auch nutzergenerierte Inhalte (Tags, Kommentare, Bewertungen).

Das Konzept der informationalen Ökosysteme nach KERRES & HEINEN (2015) stellt eine explizite Verbindung zur Open-Education-Bewegung her und bildet daher eine zentrale Basis für unser Theorieverständnis. Da auch Studierende im Zuge der zunehmenden Bedeutung von digitalen Kompetenzen, im Sinne auch von instrumentellen Fertigkeiten und Wissen über die Nutzung von Technologien (SEUFERT, GUGGEMOS, TARANTINI & SCHUMANN, 2019), vermehrt in non-formalen und informellen Kontexten ihre Kompetenzen entwickeln, ist zudem die Verbindung von formalem, non-formalem und informellem Lernen (vgl. SEDITA, 2003) ein zentrales Element unserer Konzeption eines offenen Lernökosystems im digitalen Bildungsraum der Hochschule. Die Selbstorganisation von Akteurinnen/Akteuren in einer gemeinschaftsähnlichen Organisation betonen alle vorliegenden Ansätze. Wir sehen das als eine erfolgversprechende Perspektive, um insbesondere in Co-Creation-Prozessen die nachhaltige Weiterentwicklung von Bildungsdienstleistungen sicherzustellen. Fehlend bislang ist allen Konzeptionen, wie bedeutend Ökosysteme für die Nutzung von Big Data und künstlicher Intelligenz (KI) künftig sein werden. Aus unserer Sicht stellen sie eine zentrale Voraussetzung dar, um KI-basierte Bildungsdienstleistungen entwickeln zu können, da hierzu große Datenmengen erforderlich sind.

3.2 Entwicklungsstufen der digitalen Transformation

Aufbauend auf dem erarbeiteten Grundverständnis von offenen Lernökosystemen in der Hochschulbildung möchten wir nach Entwicklungsstufen bzw. nach zwei Wellen der Digitalisierung nach WAHLSTER (2017) unterscheiden. Bei der ersten Welle der Digitalisierung geht es dabei um maschinen*lesbare* Daten sowie Internet- und Cloudtechnologien, bei der zweiten Welle um maschinen*verstehbare* Daten sowie KI und maschinelles Lernen (Digitalisierung „mit Sinn und Verstand", WAHLSTER, 2017, S. 11). Bei der digitalen Transformation der Hochschulbildung geht es daher darum, diese Entwicklungsstufen zu verstehen und für die Qualitätsentwicklung der Hochschulbildung zu nutzen.

Für die Organisationsentwicklung haben sich in diesem Zusammenhang Reifegradmodelle etabliert, die anhand von konstituierenden Merkmalen Entwicklungsstufen für die gewünschte Transformation definieren. Das macht die Entwicklung fassbar und dadurch besser plan- und steuerbar, während die langfristigen Entwicklungsziele im Blick behalten werden (SCHALLMO et al., 2017). Die Entwicklungsstufen in Abb. 2 basieren auf der empirischen Arbeit zuhanden des SBFI (SEUFERT, 2018) und der differenzierten anschließenden Deliberation (SEUFERT, GUGGEMOS & TARANTINI, 2018). Durch diese Entwicklungsstufen wird der Prozess hin zu einem Ökosystem, das formales, non-formales und informelles Lernen und damit die Verbindung zu Open Education herstellt, aufgezeigt.

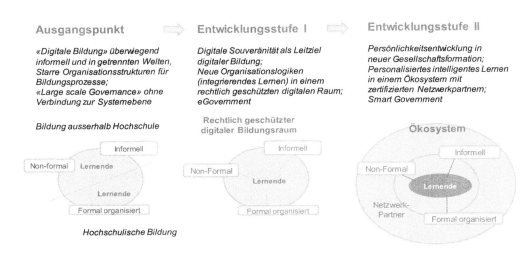

Abb. 2: Entwicklungsstufen der digitalen Transformation in Hochschulen
(SEUFERT, 2018, S. 53)

Ausgangspunkt: Neue Ziele und Inhalte für die digitale Hochschulbildung

Studierende an Hochschulen erwerben bislang digitale Kompetenzen überwiegend in informellen Kontexten. Bildungsprozesse finden im Hochschulkontext nach einer curricularen Programmlogik statt. Dabei existieren derzeit zahlreiche Bestrebungen, neue Ziele und Inhalte in bestehende Curricula zu integrieren, wie OBLINGER (2018) argumentiert:

- Künstliche Intelligenz, maschinelles Lernen, Datenmanagement,
- Kompetenzen in Mathematik und Statistik (mit Blick auf die in vielen Berufsfeldern erforderlichen Datenanalysen),
- Ethisches Handeln und Entscheiden (‚digitale Ethik‘), z. B. auf der Grundlage maschineller Datenauswertungen,
- Fachübergreifende Kompetenzen wie z. B. kritisches Denken, funktionsübergreifende Zusammenarbeit und Teamarbeit sowie neue Metakompe-

tenzen wie Computational Thinking (WING, 2006) als Element der informatischen Bildung.

Strukturen und Kulturen in der Hochschulbildung sind eher noch starr. Geschlossene Lernplattformen und die Qualitätsentwicklung als ein isoliertes Handlungsfeld sind häufig innovationshinderlich.

Entwicklungsstufe I: Flexible Organisationslogiken und Innovationskulturen

Bei wachsender Heterogenität der Studierendenschaft sowie einer Vielfalt an Kompetenzen, die im Laufe eines Studiums erworben werden sollen, steigt der Bedarf an individueller Beratung. Hierauf kann reagiert werden, indem Wahlmöglichkeiten erhöht und Kompetenzcoaching für eine individualisierte Studiengestaltung und Bildungspfade eingeführt werden. Digitale Medien bieten hier neue Möglichkeiten für ein Kompetenzcoaching im Sinne einer digitalen Lernbegleitung und personalisierten Bildung. Ein solches Coaching sollte eine kontinuierliche Reflexion der individuellen Ziele, der bisher erworbenen Fähigkeiten sowie des weiteren Bildungswegs ermöglichen. Der Lernende rückt somit in das Zentrum der Hochschulbildung, um formales, non-formales und informelles Lernen zu verknüpfen.

Hochschulen ermöglichen Studierenden ein hohes Maß an Flexibilität durch abgestimmte Präsenz- und Onlinephasen (Blended-Learning-Formate). Analoge Lernerfahrungen auf dem Campus können künftig durch digitale Medien sinnvoll ergänzt werden (z. B. durch virtuelle Lernräume oder Augmented Reality, Community Building in Onsite-Veranstaltungen). Berufliche Kompetenzprofile ändern sich mit zunehmender Geschwindigkeit und umfassender als bisher. Daher gewinnt die wissenschaftliche Weiterbildung an Hochschulen und damit verknüpft das lebenslange akademische Lernen an Bedeutung. Neue Weiterbildungsformate wie MOOCs bieten auf diesem Gebiet flexibel nutzbare Angebote.

Entwicklungsstufe II: Personalisiertes, intelligentes Lernen in Ökosystemen

Die Einbeziehung verschiedener Lernorte durch Kooperationen mit Praxispartnerinnen/-partnern, anderen Hochschulen und Bildungsanbieterinnen/-anbietern kann eine stärkere Individualisierung von Studiengängen als bisher ermöglichen. Neue Lernräume in Form von Design Thinking Labs, Zukunftslabs, Social Impact Labs und ähnlichen Einrichtungen kollaborativen Lernens und Arbeitens können ‚Biotope für Neues' sein und einer neuen und breiten ‚Open Innovation'-Kultur den Weg bereiten.

Integriertes Lernen bzw. Blended Learning erhält eine neue Brisanz. Studierende sind permanent online, auch auf dem Campus. Lernen trotz digitaler Medien ist somit von Relevanz. Auch aufgrund einer zunehmenden Heterogenität ergeben sich die Anforderungen an eine stärkere Individualisierung und Personalisierung. Während Individualisierung primär durch die Dozierenden gesteuert wird, passende Lerninhalte, Lernaktivitäten und Unterstützung bereitzustellen, bedeutet Personalisierung im engeren Sinne, dass die Lernenden selbst auswählen, welche Lernziele, Lerninhalte und Lernaktivitäten sie bearbeiten möchten und welche Art von Unterstützung und Beurteilung sie sich dabei wünschen (BRAY & MCCLASKEY, 2015; STEBLER, PAULI & REUSSER, 2017). Nach McLOUGHLIN & LEE (2010) sollte die Personalisierung von Lernumgebungen auch beinhalten, dass Lernende darin unterstützt werden, fundamentale Kompetenzen auszubilden, um ihr eigenes Lernen managen zu können.

Vor diesem Hintergrund stellt sich die Frage, welche Rolle die digitalen Medien sowie die Entwicklungen im Bereich der Digitalisierung, insbesondere Learning Analytics, in personalisierten Lernansätzen spielen. Ziel dabei ist es, jedem Individuum einen persönlichen Zugang und Empfehlungen z. B. für Lernpfade auf der Basis von KI zu ermöglichen. Die entsprechenden Skaleneffekte, um entsprechende Trainingsdaten für die Entwicklung KI-basierter Lernumgebungen zu gewinnen, sind nur in einer Netzwerk- bzw. Plattformökonomie zu erzielen (DILLENBOURG, 2016). Für die Anwendung von Data Science im Bildungsbereich sind daher offene Lernökosysteme von zentraler Bedeutung.

Open Educational Resources in offenen Lernsystemen können in einem Ökosystem kontinuierlich verbessert werden. Co-Creation-Prozesse zwischen Lernenden und Lehrenden bzw. Forschenden tragen dazu bei, dass Bildungsprozesse verbessert und neue Lehr-Lernkulturen etabliert werden können. Vor dem Hintergrund des schnellen Wandels kann die Aktualität der Lernmaterialien besser sichergestellt werden als bei klassischen statischen Lehrmitteln. Zudem können mit Learning Analytics Auswertungen (z. B. Abschneiden der Lernenden bei Quizzes oder Abbruch von Lernprozessen) und Echtzeit-Feedback generiert werden, um damit ebenfalls schneller und effektiver Lehrmaterialien zu verbessern.

Dateninfrastrukturen können aufgebaut werden, um mittels Learning Analytics pädagogische Interventionen kontinuierlich zu verbessern. Qualitätsentwicklung wird somit zu einem integrierten Handlungsfeld in einem digitalen Ökosystem der Hochschulbildung.

4 Fallbeispiel für den Aufbau von offenen Ökosystemen – Digital Israel National Initiative

Auf der Ebene des Bildungssystems (Makro-Ebene) stellt derzeit die nationale Initiative ‚Digital Israel' ein herausragendes Fallbeispiel dar. Das Vorhaben leistet einen Beitrag zur Weiterentwicklung des Bildungssystems, indem ein Ökosystem im Bildungsbereich geschaffen werden soll. Die Hochschulen fungieren dabei als eine treibende Kraft, um Bildungsangebote für das offene Lernökosystem zu entwickeln (SPIGELMAN, 2015). Das Fallbeispiel ist im Gesamtkontext der wirtschaftlichen Entwicklungen in Israel zu sehen. Innovative Technologien in den Bereichen Cyber- und Informationssicherheit, Fintech, Smart Cities, Gesundheit und Bildung stehen im Vordergrund der Initiative. Nach SPIGELMAN (2015, S. 10) ist dabei ein Leitziel „to foster the growth of digital industries in Israel, to support the development of an innovation ecosystem, to improve and integrate the digital revolution in government work and the public domain, and to foster and help citizens and businesses exploit the advantages of ICT technologies and data driven innovation".

An anderer Stelle (SPIGELMAN, S. 46) wird die Bedeutung der Förderung eines „Startup Ecosystem" von staatlicher Seite her (z. B. in Form von Inkubatoren) herausgestellt: „Strengthening Israel's standing as an advanced innovative country, a startup ecosystem, will create significant benefits for the economy and for narrowing gaps, improving public goods and increasing opportunities for the public at large". Öffentliche Bildungsgüter in der Rahmung offener Lernökosytemene in Co-Creation-Prozessen mit Universitäten, Studierenden, Lehrenden sowie öffentlichen Bildungseinrichtungen bereitzustellen und deren Nachhaltigkeit sicherzustellen, ist ein erklärtes Ziel von ‚Digital Israel'.

Israel hat im Rahmen dieses nationalen Programmes, das auch unter dem Namen ‚No One Left Behind' firmiert, das Ministerium for Social Equality gegründet. Gleichberechtigte Chancen auf Bildung sind damit das erklärte Ziel der Digitalisierungsinitiative. Campus.il fungiert dabei als die nationale MOOC-Plattform (basierend auf Open edX). Die Lehrpersonen auf der Sekundarstufe I sind dazu verpflichtet, mit den Lernenden pro Semester mindestens einen MOOC im Unterricht zu bearbeiten, um sie auf ein lebenslanges Lernen im digitalen Ökosystem vorzubereiten. Die Kurse orientieren sich am P21 21st century skills framework[2].

---

[2] Weitere Informationen sind zu finden unter http://www.battelleforkids.org/networks/p21

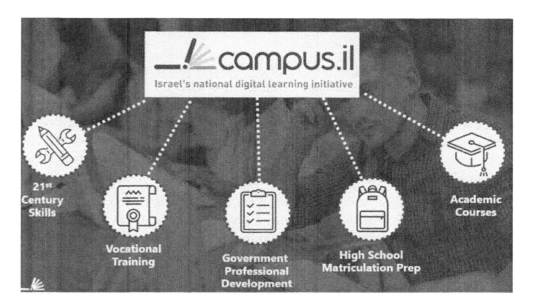

Abb. 3: Campus IL-Initiative in Israel (IBL, 2018)

5 Fazit und Ausblick

Die digitale Transformation stellt derzeit die Hochschulbildung vor eine große Herausforderung. Befinden sich derzeit die meisten Hochschulen in der ersten Welle der Digitalisierung, d. h. in der Digitalisierung von Prozessen, so ist in Konturen bereits eine zweite Welle (insbesondere durch Big Data und KI) zu erkennen. Für die Nutzbarmachung der Potenziale dieser Entwicklungen scheinen Geschäfts- bzw. Funktionsmodelle der Netzwerkökonomie, wie es Ökosysteme und Plattformökonomien darstellen, besonders zukunftsträchtig.

Aufbauend auf dem erarbeiteten Grundverständnis offener Lernökosysteme in der Hochschulbildung schlagen wir zwei Entwicklungsstufen entsprechend der Digitalisierungswellen vor. Bei der digitalen Transformation der Hochschulbildung geht es darum, diese Entwicklungsstufen zu verstehen und für die Qualitätsentwicklung der Hochschulbildung nutzbar zu machen.

Die Potenziale der Digitalisierung in einer Netzwerkökonomie haben wir im vorliegenden Beitrag herausgearbeitet. Je größer und individualisierter digitale Ökosysteme sind, umso mehr relevante Daten können für die kontinuierliche Verbesserung pädagogischer Interventionen gesammelt werden. Die permanente Interaktion und dadurch die Verschmelzung von Hochschule, Forschungsgegenstand und Lern- und Entwicklungsumgebung führen in Richtung Entwicklungsstufe II im digitalen Transformationsprozess, vgl. Abb. 2.

Der Fokus des vorliegenden Beitrags liegt auf den Potenzialen von digitalen Ökosystemen für die Hochschulbildung, um die Verbindung zu Open Education und damit die Verbindung zwischen Lernen in formal-organisierten, non-formalen und informellen Kontexten herzustellen. Neben den bereits dargestellten Herausforderungen können weitere Hindernisse und Schwierigkeiten den Aufbau funktionsfähiger digitaler Ökosysteme erschweren. Hierzu wäre weitere Forschung nötig.

Insbesondere die Gewährleistung des Datenschutzes in offenen, kollaborativen Systemen wird zur Herausforderung und bedarf technischer und politisch-rechtlicher Antworten, die sich nicht auf nationale Wirkungsräume beschränken. Zudem könnte ein zu starkes Konkurrenzdenken den Aufbau von Ökosystemen behindern. Wenn die relevanten Akteurinnen/Akteure primär Gefahren statt Chancen in der Kollaboration sehen, beeinträchtigt das die Entwicklung und eine effiziente Nutzung von offenen Systemen.

6 Literaturverzeichnis

Bahr, F., Dapp, T. F., Dobusch, L., Grzegorzek, M., Kerst, V., Meineberg, R. et al. (2012). *Schönes neues Internet? Chancen und Risiken für Innovation in digitalen Ökosystemen.* Policy Brief, 05/12. Berlin: Stiftung neue Verantwortung.

Bauer, W., Schlund, S., Marrenbach, D. & Ganschar, O. (2014). *Industrie 4.0 - Volkswirtschaftliches Potenzial für Deutschland.* Berlin: BITKOM Studie. https://www.produktionsarbeit.de/content/dam/produktionsarbeit/de/documents/Studie-Industrie-4-0-Volkswirtschaftliches-Potential-fuer-Deutschland.pdf

Bellmann, L. (2017). Digitalisierung kaufmännischer Prozesse, Veränderungen des Profils von kaufmännischen Tätigkeiten und Qualifikationsanforderungen. In K. Wilbers (Hrsg.), *Industrie 4.0: Herausforderung für die kaufmännische Berufsbildung* (S. 53-66). Berlin: Epubli.

Blossfeld, H.-P., Bos, W., Daniel, H.-D., Hannover, B., Köller, O., Lenzen, D. et al. (2018). *Digitale Souveränität und Bildung. Gutachten des Aktionsrats Bildung.* Münster: Waxmann.

Brahm, T., Jenert, T. & Euler, D. (2016). *Pädagogische Hochschulentwicklung. Von der Programmatik zur Implementierung.* Wiesbaden: Springer.

Bray, B. & McClaskey, K. (2015). *Make learning personal: The what, who, wow, where, and why.* Thousand Oaks, CA: Corwin Press.

Chang, V. & Guetl, C. (2007). E-Learning Ecosystem (ELES) – A Holistic Approach for the Development of more Effective Learning Environment for Small-and-Medium Sized Enterprises (SMEs). *Digital EcoSystems and Technologies Conference, Cairns, Australia.* https://doi.org/10.1109/DEST.2007.372010

Dahlstrom, E., Brooks, C. D. & Bichsel, J. (2014). The Current Ecosystem of Learning Management Systems in Higher Education: Student, Faculty, and IT Perspectives. *Technical Report EDUCAUSE.* https://doi.org/10.13140/RG.2.1.3751.6005

Dillenbourg, P. (2016). The Evolution of Research on Digital Education. *International Journal of Artificial Intelligence in Education, 26*(2), 544-560. https://doi.org/10.1007/s40593-016-0106-z

Dittler, U. (2017). Ein kurzer historischer Rückblick auf die bisherigen drei Wellen des E-Learning. In U. Dittler (Hrsg.), *E-Learning 4.0. Mobile Learning, Lernen mit Smart Devices und Lernen in sozialen Netzwerken* (S. 5-42). Berlin: De Gruyter.

Galarneau, L. (2005). Spontaneous Communities of Learning: A Social Analysis of Learning Ecosystems in Massively Multiplayer Online Gaming (MMOG) Environments. *Digital Games Research Conference, Changing Views: Worlds in Play, Vancouver, British Columbia, Canada*, SSRN Electronic Journal. https://doi.org/10.2139/ssrn.810064

Getto, B., Hintze, P. & Kerres, M. (2018). (Wie) Kann Digitalisierung zur Hochschulentwicklung beitragen? In B. Getto, P. Hintze, & M. Kerres (Hrsg.), *Digitalisierung und Hochschulentwicklung. Proceedings zur 26. Tagung der Gesellschaft für Medien in der Wissenschaft e.V.* (S. 13-25). Münster: Waxmann.

Hofhues, S. & Schiefner-Rohs, M. (2017). Vom Labor zum medialen Bildungsraum. Hochschul- und Mediendidaktik nach Bologna. In C. Igel (Hrsg.), *Bildungsräume. Proceedings der 25. Jahrestagung der Gesellschaft für Medien in der Wissenschaft, 5. bis 8. September 2017 in Chemnitz* (S. 32-43). Münster: Waxmann.

IBL (2018). *Campus-IL, Israel's National Open edX Platform, Consolidates Its Project.* https://iblnews.org/2018/08/02/

Kerres, M. (2016). E-Learning vs. Digitalisierung der Bildung: Neues Label oder neues Paradigma? In A. Hohenstein & K. Wilbers (Hrsg.), *Handbuch E-Learning*. Köln: Fachverlag Deutscher Wirtschaftsdienst. 61. Ergänzungslieferung.

Kerres, M. & Getto, B. (2015). Vom E-Learning Projekt zur nachhaltigen Hochschulentwicklung: Strategisches 25 Alignment im Kernprozess „Studium & Lehre". In A. Mai (Hrsg.), *Hochschulwege 2015. Wie verändern Projekte die Hochschulen?* Dokumentation der Tagung in Weimar am 8.-9. März 2015. Weimar.

Kerres, M. & Heinen, R. (2014). Open educational resources and informational ecosystems: Edutags as a connector for open learning. Friesen, N., Hug, T. & Meister, D. (Hrsg.), *MedienPädagogik. Zeitschrift für Theorie und Praxis der Medienbildung, 24* (Themenheft: Educational Media Ecologies), 154-173.

Kerres, M. & Heinen, R. (2015). Open Informational Ecosystems: The missing link for sharing resources for education. *The International Review of Research in Open and Distributed Learning*, 16(1), 24-39. http://www.irrodl.org/index.php/irrodl/article/view/2008

Looi, C. K. (2001). Enhancing learning ecology on the Internet. *Journal of Computer Assisted Learning, 17*, 13-20. https://doi.org/10.1111/j.1365-2729.2001.00155.x

McLoughlin, C. & Lee, M. J. W. (2010). Personalisation and self regulated learning in the Web 2.0 era: International exemplars of innovative pedagogy using social software. *Australasian Journal of Educational Technology, 26*(1), 28-43.

Mormann, H. & Willjes, K. (2013). Organisationsprojekt und Projektorganisation. In F. Stratmann (Hrsg.), *IT und Organisation in Hochschulen* (S. 23-42). Hannover: HIS GmbH.

Oblinger, D. (2018). *Smart Machines and Human Expertise: Challenges for Higher Education. EDUCAUSE Review, 53*(5). https://er.educause.edu/~/media/files/articles/2018/8/er185w.pdfl?la=en

Östereich, B. & Schröder, C. (2017). *Das kollegial geführte Unternehmen. Ideen und Praktiken für die agile Organisation von morgen*. München: Vahlen.

Oswald, G. & Krcmar, H. (2018). *Digitale Transformation. Fallbeispiele und Branchenanalysen.* Wiesbaden: Springer Gabler. https://doi.org/10.1007/978-3-658-22624-4

Pousttchi, K. (2018). *Digitale Transformation. Enzyklopädie der Wirtschaftsinformatik.* http://www.enzyklopaedie-der-wirtschaftsinformatik.de/lexikon/technologien-methoden/Informatik--Grundlagen/digitalisierung/digitale-transformation

Schallmo, D., Rusnjak, A., Anzengruber, J., Werani, T. & Jünger, M. (2017). *Digitale Transformation von Geschäftsmodellen. Grundlagen, Instrumente und Best Practices*. Wiesbaden: Springer.

Schneider, M. & Preckel, F. (2017). Variables Associated With Achievement in Higher Education: A Systematic Review of Meta-Analyses. *Psychological Bulletin. Advance online publication.* https://doi.org/10.1037/bul0000098

Schirmers, L., Schröder, J., Sönmez, N. A. & Weihmann, S. (2016). *Hochschulbildung für die Arbeitswelt 4.0. Jahresbericht 2016.* Stifterverband für die Deutsche Wissenschaft e.V. (Hrsg.). https://www.stifterverband.org/medien/hochschul-bildungs-report-2020-bericht-2016

Seufert, S. (2018). *Flexibilisierung der Berufsbildung im Kontext fortschreitender Digitalisierung.* Bericht im Auftrag des Staatssekretariats für Bildung, Forschung und Innovation SBFI im Rahmen des Projekts „Berufsbildung 2030 – Vision und Strategische Leitlinien". Verfügbar unter https://www.sbfi.admin.ch/sbfi/de/home/bildung/berufsbildungssteuerung-und--politik/projekte-und-initiativen/berufsbildungsstrategie-2030.html

Seufert, S., Ebner, M., Kopp, M. & Schlass, B. (2015). Editorial: E-Learning-Strategien für die Hochschullehre. *Zeitschrift für Hochschulentwicklung, 10*(2). https://www.zfhe.at/index.php/zfhe/article/view/843

Seufert, S., Guggemos, J. & Tarantini, E. (2018). Digitale Transformation in Schulen – Kompetenzanforderungen an Lehrpersonen. *Beiträge zur Lehrerinnen- und Lehrerbildung, 36*(2), 175-193.

Seufert, S., Guggemos, J., Tarantini, E. & Schumann, S. (2019). Professionelle Kompetenzen von Lehrpersonen im Kontext des digitalen Wandels – Entwicklung eines Rahmenkonzepts und Validierung in der kaufmännischen Domäne. *Zeitschrift für Berufs- und Wirtschaftspädagogik, 115*(2), 312-339. https://doi.org/10.25162/zbw-2019-00013

Spigelman, S.-L. (2015). *The Digital Israel National Initiative: The National Digital Program of the Government of Israel.* https://www.gov.il/BlobFolder/news/digital_israel_national_plan/en/The%20National%20Digital%20Program%20of%20the%20Government%20of%20Israel.pdf

Stebler, R., Pauli, C. & Reusser, K. (2017). Personalisiertes Lernen – Chancen und Herausforderungen für Lehrpersonen. *Lehren & Lernen, 43*(5), 21-28.

Wahlster, W. (2017). Künstliche Intelligenz als Treiber der zweiten Digitalisierungswelle. *IM+io Das Magazin für Innovation, Organisation und Management.* http://www.wolfgang-wahlster.de/wordpress/wp-content/uploads/KI_als_Treiber_der_zweiten_Digitalisierungswelle.pdf

Wing, J. M. (2006). Computational thinking. *Communications of the ACM, 49*(3), 33-35. https://doi.org/10.1145/1118178.1118215

Autorin/Autoren

Prof. Dr. Sabine SEUFERT || Universität St. Gallen || Guisantstr. 1a, CH-9010 St. Gallen

https://iwp-digital-betrieb.unisg.ch

sabine.seufert@unisg.ch

Dr. Josef GUGGEMOS, MBR || Universität St. Gallen || Guisantstr. 1a, CH-9010 St. Gallen

https://iwp-digital-betrieb.unisg.ch

josef.guggemos@unisg.ch

Luca MOSER, M.A. || Universität St. Gallen || Guisantstr. 1a, CH-9010 St. Gallen

https://iwp-digital-betrieb.unisg.ch

luca.moser@unisg.ch

Christian HELBIG[1] & Bence LUKÁCS

Openness als Prinzip von Organisationsentwicklung. Werkbericht zu partizipationsorientierten Dialogformaten im Projekt OERlabs

Zusammenfassung

Ziel des BMBF-Projekts OERlabs war es, einen Kulturwandel in Lehre und Forschung hin zu offenen Praktiken anzustoßen. Hierfür wurden Akteurinnen/Akteure entlang der Lehrer*innenbildungskette im Rahmen von Multi-Stakeholder-Dialogen selbst mit offenen Bildungspraktiken konfrontiert, um partizipatorisch Herausforderungen und Lösungen für die Implementation von OER (Open Educational Resources) an der Hochschule (bzw. der Lehrer*innenbildung) zu be- und erarbeiten. Der folgende Werkstattbericht beschreibt die Potenziale von Open Education für organisationales Lernen sowie die Implementierung offener Bildungspraktiken im Rahmen von Dialogformaten.

Schlüsselwörter

Open Education, partizipatorische Hochschulentwicklung, Organisationsentwicklung, Lehrentwicklung, Open Educational Practices

---

[1] E-Mail: christian.helbig@uni-koeln.de

Openness as a principle of organisational development in educational contexts: Workshop report on participation-oriented dialogue formats in the OERlabs project

Abstract

The aim of the BMBF-funded project OERlabs was to initiate a cultural transformation in teaching and research towards open practices. For this purpose, actors in teacher education were confronted with open educational practices within the framework of multi-stakeholder dialogues, in order to develop challenges and solutions for the advancement of OER (Open Educational Resources) in teacher education (as well as the university). This workshop report describes the potential of Open Education for organisational learning, as well as the implementation of open-educational practices within the framework of dialogue formats.

Keywords

open education, participatory development, organisational development, teaching development, open educational practices

1 Kulturelle Herausforderungen bei der Etablierung offener Praktiken in Hochschulen

Der bildungsphilosophische Anspruch offener Bildungspraktiken ist es, den Zugang zu Bildung(sressourcen) vollständig zu öffnen und eine selbstgesteuerte Auseinandersetzung mit und Aneignung von Welt zu fördern, unabhängig von ökonomischen Status und sozialer Herkunft der Lernenden (DEIMANN, 2018, S. 15). Open Science bzw. Open Research übertragen dies auf Prozesse von Wissenschaft und Forschung. Digitale Technologien bieten dafür die strukturellen Voraussetzungen. Sie sind aber nicht hinreichend, solange sie nicht mit anschlussfähigen didaktischen Ansätzen, Forschungskonzepten und Publikationsstrategien verknüpft werden.

Wenngleich es in der Diskussion um einen tiefgreifenden Kulturwandel in allen Bildungsbereichen geht, der grundsätzliche Haltungen und Entwicklungsprozesse hin zu offenen Bildungspraktiken erfordert, liegt der Kern von Open Education häufig auf Ebene von Produkten, die als Open Educational Ressources (OER) und Open Access (OA) verhandelt werden (MAYRBERGER &THIEMANN, 2018). Dies ist dann nachvollziehbar, wenn die Auffindbarkeit und der Zugang zu Bildungsmaterialien und Forschungsergebnissen im Vordergrund stehen. Mit Blick auf Hochschulen und Forschung ist die Diskussion um OER und OA allerdings verknüpft mit kulturellen Herausforderungen des Wissenschaftsbetriebs: Reputation ist an exklusive Publikationsstrategien geknüpft. Folge ist u. a. eine fehlende intrinsische Motivation zu Open Education, während die Möglichkeiten zur Publikation als OER und OA zunehmen (WELLER, 2014). Hinzukommen Herausforderungen der organisationalen Rahmenbedingungen an Hochschulen, die als lose gekoppelte Expertenorganisationen (PELLERT, 1999) beschrieben werden können. Darin ist eingeschrieben, dass die professionelle Identität von Lehrenden und Forschenden an Hochschulen häufig an die disziplinäre Sozialisation geknüpft ist und weniger an die jeweilige Hochschule (EULER, 2018, S. 772). In diesem Zusammenhang stehen nicht zuletzt auch begrenzte Bestrebungen und Räume zur inter- und transdisziplinären Kooperation und Kollaboration, die über die akademische Selbstverwaltung hinausgehen. Die Etablierung offener Bildungspraktiken an Hochschulen, die meist unabhängig von Disziplinen verhandelt werden, wird dadurch erschwert.

Es drängt sich die Frage auf, wie ein Kulturwandel in Lehre und Forschung hin zu offenen Bildungs- und Forschungspraktiken an Hochschulen angestoßen werden kann und – so soll hier erweitert werden – welche Rolle die aktive Auseinandersetzung mit offenen Bildungspraktiken bei diesem Prozess selbst haben kann. Das Projekt OERlabs nahm sich diesen Fragestellungen an und bearbeitete sie mit Hilfe von Multi-Stakeholder Dialogen (MSD) (DODDS & BENSON, 2013). Gegenstand der MSD waren die kooperative und kollaborative Entwicklung von Lösungen für die Implementation von OER in der Lehrer*innenausbildung. Hinführend zur Beschreibung der Ergebnisse und Erfahrungen zu partizipationsorientierten Dialogformaten im Projekt OERlabs wird im Folgenden Kulturwandel an Hochschule als organisationales Lernen beschrieben und Dialogformate theoretisch mit den Prämissen offener Bildungspraktiken verknüpft. Abschließend wird dargelegt, wie die Prinzipien von Open Education zu Aspekten von Organisationsentwicklung in Bildungskontexten weiterentwickelt werden können.

2 Kulturwandel an Hochschulen verstanden als organisationales Lernen

Die Rahmenbedingungen und Prinzipien von Innovations- und Veränderungsprozessen an Hochschulen sind Gegenstand organisationspädagogischer Fragestellungen (EULER, 2018). Hochschulen, verstanden als lernende Organisationen, besitzen demnach die Potenziale, Fehler zu identifizieren und zu bearbeiten sowie neue Problemlösungs- und Handlungsfähigkeiten zu schaffen, indem Veränderungen in der organisationalen Wert- und Wissensbasis angestoßen werden (SCHÖNWALD, 2007, S. 34). Zwei Dimensionen sind zentral (GÖHLICH, 2018, S. 374):

1. Handlungspraktiken in Organisationen sind abhängig vom impliziten Wissen über legitimierte Praktiken und Entscheidungen der einzelnen Mitglieder. Organisationales Lernen bedeutet demnach Reflexionsangebote zu schaffen, in denen die Vorstellungen und Möglichkeiten von Organisation und daran orientierte Handlungspraktiken überprüft und modifiziert werden können.
2. Organisationales Lernen erfordert Zeiten und Räume im organisationalen Alltag, in denen der Austausch von Praxisgemeinschaften sowie die Vergewisserung, Reflexion und Bearbeitung von Praxismustern gefördert wird.

Mit Blick auf offene Bildungspraktiken können beide Dimensionen nicht losgelöst voneinander verhandelt werden, zumal der Einsatz von offenen Bildungsmaterialien, die Förderung von Kollaboration und Vernetzung der Lernenden sowie die Verknüpfung von Open Education und Forschungspraxis voraussetzungsvoll sind.

Auf der Ebene einzelner Lehrender braucht es Wissen und Erfahrungen zu OER und (medien-)didaktische Konzepte offener Bildung, die kollaborativ und reflexiv entwickelt werden. Folgerichtig gilt es Formate an Hochschulen zu verankern, in denen Wissen zu offenen Bildungspraktiken gefördert und Erfahrungen mit ihrem Umgang ausgetauscht werden können.

Zudem kann die Etablierung offener Bildungspraktiken an Hochschulen in Anlehnung an die Diffusionstheorie (ROGERS, 2003) beschrieben werden. Demnach gewinnt eine Innovation (ein neues Produkt, eine neue Technologie oder eine neue soziale Praxis) an gesellschaftlicher Bedeutung, wenn ausreichend viele Menschen die Innovation angenommen haben. Dieser Prozess ist abhängig von der Beschaffenheit der Innovation, den Kommunikationskanälen und zeitlichen Dimensionen. Mit Blick auf Hochschulen bedeutet dies, dass die Etablierung von offenen Bildungspraktiken abhängig ist von der wiederkehrenden (Zeit) aktiven Auseinandersetzung (Beschaffenheit) und der sozialen Interaktion bzw. dem Erfahrungsaustausch über das Thema (Kommunikation).

3 Partizipationsorientierte Dialogformate als Nukleus offener Bildungspraktiken

Beide Perspektiven – Hochschule als lernende Organisation (GÖHLICH, 2018) und die Diffusion von Innovation (ROGERS, 2003) – schreiben der sozialen Interaktion eine gewichtige Rolle bei der Etablierung neuer Idee und Konzepte in gefestigten Strukturen zu. Ebenso sind die internationalen Diskussionen um Open Education an diese theoretischen Konzepte anknüpfungsfähig (INAMORATO DOS SANTOS, 2017, S. 23).

Die Einbindung relevanter Akteurinnen/Akteure und die kollaborative Auseinandersetzung ist demnach nicht nur als Aspekt von Organisationsentwicklung hin zu Open Education zu verstehen, sondern als ein *Kernelement*. Aus diesen Verständnisweisen lassen sich Überlegungen für die didaktische Begleitung von Organisationsentwicklungsprozessen ableiten:

- Gegenstand und Methode von Organisationsentwicklungen sollten kohärent sein (der Weg hinzu Offenheit erfordert Offenheit).
- Open Education setzt sich stets aus Kollaboration und einer Kultur des Teilens zusammen.
- Die Teil*gabe* an Gestaltungsprozessen soll für alle Teilnehmenden gleichermaßen möglich sind, d. h. Hierarchiestrukturen sollten zumindest zeitweise gelockert oder gegebenenfalls ausgegliedert werden.
- Die Zielstellung sollte kollaborativ entwickelt werden, z. B. mit Hilfe von Positionspapieren bzw. der Möglichkeit, eigene Erfahrungen und Perspektiven offen zu kommunizieren.

Eine Möglichkeit der Initiierung und Umsetzung offener Hochschulentwicklungsprozesse stellen partizipationsorientierte Dialogformate dar. Als sog. Multi-Stakeholder-Dialoge (MSD) zielen diese Formate darauf ab, aufgaben- und hierarchieübergreifend Vertreter/innen unterschiedlicher Arbeits- und Aufgabenbereiche sowie Hierarchieebenen einer Organisation in Austausch zu bringen, um sowohl Potenziale als auch Herausforderungen von Innovationen zu identifizieren, zu reflektieren und konsensfähige Lösungswege für konkrete Problemstellungen zu entwickeln (DODDS & BENSON, 2013).

4 Dialogorientierte Umsetzung im Projekt OERlabs

Offene Bildungspraktiken beinhalten im Kern Offenheit, Kommunikation und Kollaboration – diese Prinzipien lassen sich allerdings nicht fließend in Arbeitsprozesse und -strukturen einer Organisation übertragen. Mit den OERlabs wurde versucht, diese Prinzipien an der *Universität zu Köln* in einen Dialogprozess einzuarbeiten und die Teil*nehmer/innen* zu Teil*geberinnen*/Teil*gebern* werden zu lassen. Im folgenden Abschnitt wird die praktische Umsetzung der Dialogreihe beschrieben, sowie im Kontext der Gegebenheiten an der Universität zu Köln und des Projektes OERlabs eingebettet.

4.1 OpenLab und Virtuelle Arbeitsphasen

Die gesamte Projektlaufzeit der OERlabs war durch verschiedene Dialog-Formate gekennzeichnet (siehe Grafik 1): verbindliche Termine (schwarz), offene Formate (blau) und digitale bzw. Online-Termine (orange). In den OERlabs wurden verschiedene *Räume* in die Arbeitsprozesse integriert. Stakeholder, die Strategien und Lösungen zu Diskussionsthemen beitragen wollten, waren angehalten, sich digitale Tools zu erarbeiten und anzueignen. Um die Partizipation weiterer Stakeholder zu erhöhen, wurden zusätzlich papierbasierte Beteiligungsformate in Umlauf gebracht. Neben der Erwartung einer verstärkten Teilnahme möglichst heterogener Personengruppen war daran auch die Hoffnung geknüpft, dass sich Hochschulmitglieder mit weniger Interesse an digitalen Formaten den Themen rund um Openness nähern. Daran anknüpfend wurden zudem praxisorientierte *OpenLabs* veranstaltet, in denen sich Interessierte mit Themenstellungen rund um OER beschäftigen konnten, wie z. B. mit einer internationalen Perspektive zur OER-Verwendung in der Lehre oder mit der OER-Arbeit in Schulklassen.

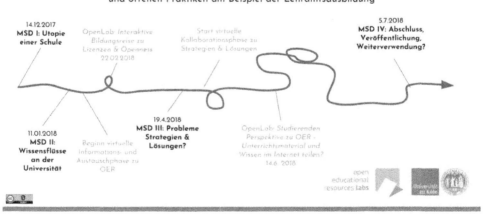

Abb. 1: Flussdiagramm des MSD-Prozess „Gute Lehre meets OER" (2017)

4.2 Ergebnisse der Dialogformate

Das Ziel des Start-Dialogs war nicht die Entwicklung von Lösungen zu konkreten Problemstellungen, sondern das Aufbrechen von Hierarchien und die Ermöglichung von Diskussionen auf Augenhöhe. Dies wurde dadurch erreicht, dass sich die unterschiedlichen Teilnehmenden in durchmischten Gruppen zu offenen Fragen (z. B. über *Zeitgemäßes Lernen*) austauschten. Zentrale Methode war das Gedankenspiel, z. B. in Form von kollaborativen Konzeptionen einer Schule auf dem Mars (ANDRASCH, 2017). Der gesamte Arbeitsprozess orientierte sich an den fünf Grundprinzipien von OER (verwahren und vervielfältigen, verwenden, verarbeiten, vermischen und verbreiten; siehe MUUSS-MERHOLZ, 2015), wodurch die Teilnehmenden bereits an offene Praktiken herangeführt wurden. Das Ergebnis war, dass alle Teilnehmenden ihre eigenen Perspektiven einbringen konnten und in der Gruppe ein Austausch über die Ausgestaltung zukünftigen Lernens stattfand. In der abschließenden Auswertung in Form von One-Minute-Papers meldeten die Teilnehmenden zurück, dass das Format etablierte Strukturen irritieren und zu neuen Ideen von Hochschule fördern konnte. Der Austausch auf Augenhöhe und die ungewöhnlichen Aufgabenstellungen wurden als innovative Methoden wahrgenommen, die unterschiedliche Erfahrungen und Wahrnehmungen der Stakeholder Rechnung tragen konnten (ausführlich siehe ANDRASCH et al., 2018).

Der anschließende Termin fokussierte thematisch Wissensmanagement und die individuellen Erfahrungen der Stakeholder. Methodisch standen die hierarchiearme Vernetzung und die Abbildung von Entwicklungsprozessen im Vordergrund. Die Beteiligten wurden motiviert den Ist- und Soll-Zustand von Wissensmanagement aus ihren Perspektiven darzustellen. Die unterschiedlichen Ansprüche, Nutzungsweisen und Erfahrungen der Stakeholdergruppen wurden bewusst einbezogen, um sowohl differenzierte Perspektiven auf digitale Wissensmanagementplattformen als auch Schnittmengen zwischen den Beteiligten transparent zu machen und zu reflektieren. Im Ergebnis standen Einsichten und Reflexionspotenziale: Vernetzungsmöglichkeiten zwischen unterschiedlichen Hierarchieebenen bzw. Stakeholder-Gruppen (z. B. zwischen Studierende und Lehrenden) sind bislang kaum vorhanden. Hier wurde eine deutliche Differenz zwischen den gemeinsam entwickelten Ist- und Soll-Zuständen festgestellt, insbesondere in Hinblick auf die Öffnung von Kommunikationsstrukturen.

Beim letzten Arbeitstermin wurden aus den Teilnehmenden Teilgebende. Im Zentrum stand die Entwicklung von Strategien und Lösungen zur Förderung von OER an Hochschulen. Die Veranstaltung wurde vom Projektteam zwar durch Methoden zur Kollaboration und Kooperation strukturiert, Kern waren aber die Erfahrungen und Meinungen der Teilgeber/innen und die Entwicklung und Präsentation von Strategien und Lösungen für reale Problemstellungen im Kontext von OER an Hochschulen. Ziel war es, die Herausforderungen und Lösungen in einer Wirkungs-Aufwand-Matrix zusammenzutragen (siehe Grafik 2). Die Ergebnisse rückten insbesondere die kulturellen Herausforderungen an Hochschulen und die Notwendigkeiten grundsätzlicher Haltungs- und Prozessänderungen hin zu offenen Bildungspraktiken in den Vordergrund. Zu den zentralen Lösungsansätzen (Initiativen aus Sicht der Teilnehmenden, die eine hohe Wirkmächtigkeit bei geringem Aufwand erwarten ließen) gehörten z. B. die Erarbeitung und Bereitstellung einer Ideensammlung (mit Blick auf OER-Lehr- und Lernmaterial), die Förderung einer Haltung des Teilens (Teilen von Wissen, Material und Methoden), die Unterstützung bzw. Vorgaben und Guidelines für Lehrkräfte bei der Verwendung von offen lizenziertem Material und die Etablierung von Open-Educational-Practices.

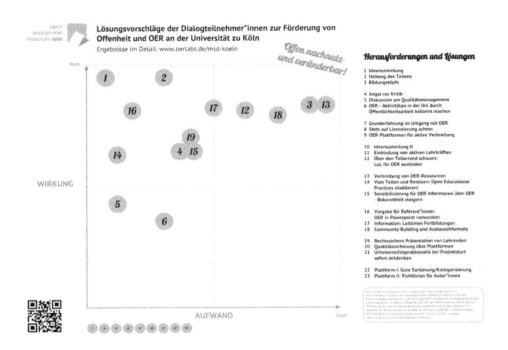

Abb. 2: Lösungsvorschläge der Dialogteilnehmer/innen zur Förderung
von Offenheit und OER an der Universität zu Köln

5 Fazit: Open Educational Practices als Prinzip von Organisationsentwicklung in Bildungskontexten

Universitäten und Hochschuleinrichtungen verstehen sich in vielen Fällen als Expertenstätten. Wie Altvater (2007) beschreibt, hat dies zur Folge, dass Organisationsentwicklung und Innovation als selbstverständlicher Prozess verstanden wird, da den genannten Institutionen sämtliche notwendigen Expertinnen/Experten be-

reits innewohnen. Dies mag grundsätzlich richtig sein, jedoch werden für zielge-
richtete und strukturierte Weiterentwicklungen Personen (bzw. Projekte) benötigt,
die diese Prozesse konzipieren, koordinieren und kontrollieren können. Zudem ist
es nach wie vor eine Herausforderung effizient und nachhaltig Lehrentwicklung zu
betreiben: Methodisch etablierten Mustern zu folgen und gleichzeitig neue Ergebnisse zu erwarten kann zu Widersprüchen und Widerständen führen. Offene Bildungspraktiken bzw. Open-Educational-Practices sollen Perspektiven erweitern,
verändern und irritieren.

Das Projekt OERlabs stellt den Versuch dar, die Bedeutung von Kollaboration im
Bildungsbereich verständlich, sicht- und greifbar darzustellen. Dabei wurde deut-
lich, dass der Kern erfolgreicher Hochschulentwicklung stets die Kollaboration,
Kooperation und Kommunikation *aller* universitärer Stakeholder ist. Mit dem Projekt OERlabs konnte eine wichtige Schnittstelle mit Blick auf die Praxis (Lehrer*innenbildungskette) gefunden werden und eine ebenso wichtige Thematik (die
Verwendung von OER) herausgehoben werden. Allerdings zeigt die tatsächliche
praktische Umsetzung dieser partizipativen Dialogreihe, dass hierbei der thematische Schwerpunkt sowie die strukturelle Ebene nicht ausschlaggebend für einen
positiven Projektverlauf und -abschluss ist, vielmehr lassen sich offene Bildungs-
formate themenunabhängig denken.

Die theoretische Auseinandersetzung und die Erfahrungen aus OERlabs geben
Hinweise darauf, dass Openness nicht nur als bildungsphilosophisches Projekt zu
verstehen ist, sondern darin Prinzipien eingelagert sind, die für die Hochschul-
bzw. Organisationsentwicklung nutzbar gemacht werden können. Partizipationsorientierte Dialogformate stellen eine Möglichkeit zur Adaption des Openness-
Gedankens in solchen Entwicklungsprozessen dar. Gemeinsame Strategieentwick-
lungen und Visionen benötigen neben Offenheit aber ebenso Mut zu Veränderung
und längerfristige Verpflichtungen zur eigenen Hochschuleinrichtung.

6   Literaturverzeichnis

Altvater, P. (2007). Organisationsberatung im Hochschulbereich – Einige Überlegungen zum Beratungsverständnis und zu Handlungsproblemen in Veränderungsprozessen. *Hochschulen, 11.*

Andrasch, M., Hofhues, S. & Lukács, B. (2018). OERlabs: Empathy first, solution later? In *4th International Conference on Higher Education Advances (HEAD'18)* (S. 1231-1238). Editorial Universitat Politècnica de València. https://doi.org/10.4995/HEAD18.2018.8182

Andrasch, M. (2017, Dezember 20). „Wie sollte eine Schule auf dem Mars aussehen?" – Auftakt des Multistakeholder-Dialogs in Köln. https://oerlabs.de/wie-sollte-eine-schule-auf-dem-mars-aussehen-auftakt-des-multistakeholder-dialogs-in-koeln/

Deimann, M. (2018). *Open Education: Auf dem Weg zu einer offenen Hochschulbildung.* transcript Verlag.

Dodds, F. & Benson, E. (2013). Multi-Stakeholder Dialogue. In *Stakeholder Forum for a Sustainable Future.* Johannesburg: Civicus.

Euler, D. (2018). Hochschulen als Orte organisationspädagogischer Forschung und Praxis. *Handbuch Organisationspädagogik, 767.*

Göhlich, M. (2018). Organisationales Lernen als zentraler Gegenstand der Organisationspädagogik. In M. Göhlich, A. Schröer & S. M. Weber (Hrsg.), *Handbuch Organisationspädagogik* (S. 365-379). Wiesbaden: Springer Fachmedien Wiesbaden. https://doi.org/10.1007/978-3-658-07512-5_3

Inamorato Dos Santos, A. (2016, Juli 27). Opening up Education: A Support Framework for Higher Education Institutions. https://ec.europa.eu/jrc/en/publication/eur-scientific-and-technical-research-reports/opening-education-support-framework-higher-education-institutions, Stand vom 14. Februar 2019.

Inamorato Dos Santos, A. (2017, Dezember 22). Going Open: Policy Recommendations on Open Education in Europe (OpenEdu Policies). https://ec.europa.eu/jrc/en/publication/eur-scientific-and-technical-research-reports/going-open-policy-recommendations-open-education-europe-openedu-policies, Stand vom 14. Februar 2019.

Mayrberger, K. & Thiemann, S. (2018). Jenseits von Selbstreferenzialität – Awareness for Openness @ UHH. In *Synergie – Fachmagazin für Digitalisierung in der Lehre* (S. 88-91). Hamburg. https://www.synergie.uni-hamburg.de/de/media/ausgabe05/synergie05-beitrag18-mayrberger-thiemann.pdf

Muus-Merholz, J. (2015, November 20). Zur Definition von „Open" in „Open Educational Resources" – die 5 R-Freiheiten nach David Wiley auf Deutsch als die 5 V-Freiheiten. https://open-educational-resources.de/5rs-auf-deutsch/, Stand vom 14. Februar 2019.

Pellert, A. (1999). *Die Universität als Organisation: die Kunst, Experten zu managen.* Böhlau Verlag Wien.

Rogers, E. M. (2003). *Diffusion of innovations.* New York: Free Press. http://books.google.com/books?id=4wW5AAAAIAAJ

Schönwald, I. (2007). *Change Management in Hochschulen: die Gestaltung soziokultureller Veränderungsprozesse zur Integration von E-Learning in die Hochschullehre.* Norderstedt: Books on Demand.

Weller, M. (2014). *The Battle for Open: How openness won and why it doesn't feel like victory.* London: Ubiquity Press. http://www.ubiquitypress.com/site/books/detail/11/battle-for-open/

Werkstattbericht

121

Autoren

Christian HELBIG ‖ Universität zu Köln, Professur für Medien-
didaktik/Medienpädagogik ‖ Gronewaldstraße 2, Postfach 53,
NRW-50931 Köln

https://www.hf.uni-koeln.de/39274

christian.helbig@uni-koeln.de

Bence LUKÁCS ‖ Universität zu Köln, Professur für Medien-
didaktik/Medienpädagogik ‖ Gronewaldstraße 2, Postfach 53,
NRW-50931 Köln

https://www.hf.uni-koeln.de/39275, https://www.bencelukacs.com

bence.lukacs@me.com

Fabian SCHUMACHER[1], Claudia MERTENS & Melanie BASTEN
(Bielefeld)

Flip the Seminar – Digitale Vorbereitung auf Praxisphasen im Lehramt

Zusammenfassung

Das Praxissemester in NRW stellt Lehramtsstudierende vor eine große Herausforderung. Begleitend zur schulischen Praxisphase müssen Studienprojekte im Sinne des Forschenden Lernens verfasst werden. Universitäre Seminare bereiten auf diese methodisch anspruchsvollen Arbeiten vor. Um den Erwerb des forschungsmethodischen Wissens zeitlich und örtlich zu flexibilisieren und den Dozierenden-Studierenden-Kontakt im Seminar zu intensivieren, wurde das Konzept des Inverted Classrooms (IC) eingeführt. Mit dem Ziel, die IC-Video-Sequenzen als OER zu veröffentlichen, wird mit einem Vor-/Nachtest-Interventions-Design mit Kontrollgruppe evaluiert, ob dieses Format u. a. motivational überlegen ist.

Schlüsselwörter

Inverted Classroom, Blended Learning, Digitales Lernen, Open Educational Ressource, Open Educational Practice

---

[1] E-Mail: fschumacher@uni-bielefeld.de

Werkstattbericht · DOI: 10.3217/zfhe-14-02/07

Flip the seminar – How to prepare students for their practice semester via digital media

Abstract

The practice semester in North Rhine-Westphalia (NRW) is a great challenge for student teachers. In addition to the practical school phase, research projects in the form of research-based learning must be completed. University seminars prepare students for these demanding tasks. The concept of the Inverted Classroom (IC) was implemented in order to make the acquisition of research methods more flexible in terms of time and place and to intensify contact between lecturer and students in the seminar. With the aim of publishing the IC video sequences as Open Educational Resources (OER), a pre/post-test-intervention design with a control group was used to evaluate if the format is superior with regard to motivation.

Keywords

Inverted Classroom, Blended Learning, Digital Learning, Open Educational Resource, Open Educational Practice

1 Ausgangslage

Eine forschend-reflexive Grundhaltung gilt als notwendige Kompetenz einer Lehrkraft (FICHTEN, 2010a; MSW, 2010). Um diese auszubilden, wurde in NRW 2015 flächendeckend ein Praxissemester als Teil der Lehrer/innenbildung eingeführt (MSW, 2010). Studierende müssen in der Praxisphase u. a. eigene Forschungsprojekte (Studienprojekte) planen und durchführen. Die hier vorgestellte Studie bezieht sich auf die fachliche Ausgestaltung in der Fachdidaktik Biologie an der Universität Bielefeld. Wichtig ist dort das gesamte Durchlaufen des Forschungszyklus nach HUBER (2009). Somit sollen die Studierenden möglichst eigenständig ein im Idealfall für Dritte interessantes Forschungsprojekt planen, durchführen und reflektieren (vgl. GROSSMANN, FRIES & WILDE, im Druck).

Problematisch für die Ausbildung der forschend-reflexiven Grundhaltung erweisen sich jedoch drei Komponenten. Als erstes sind die zeitlichen Rahmenbedingungen zu nennen, welche durch die Zulassung für den schulpraktischen Teil bestimmt werden. Hierfür müssen die Studierenden nach fünf Wochen eine erste Skizze ihres Studienprojekts abgeben und somit innerhalb kürzester Zeit dazu befähigt werden, ein theoriegeleitetes biologiedidaktisches Studienprojekt zu planen. Dieser Anforderung steht entgegen, dass die Studierenden zweitens eine mangelnde forschungsmethodische Kompetenz (RIEWERTS et al., 2018) und drittens eine wenig ausgeprägte Forschungsmotivation (vgl. FICHTEN, 2010b) aufweisen.

Um dieser Problematik zu begegnen, wurde versucht, den Studierenden über die didaktische Ausgestaltung des Seminars als „Inverted Classroom" (IC) (z. B. WEIDLICH & SPANNAGEL, 2014) eine flexiblere, verstärkt selbstgesteuerte, problemorientierte und motivierende Beschäftigung mit dem Lerngegenstand zu ermöglichen. Gleichzeitig erfüllt der Kurs Attribute einer Open Pedagogy (HEGARTY, 2015) basierend auf dem Konzept der Open Educational Practice (OEP) (vgl. EHLERS, 2011) (siehe ausführlich Kapitel 4).

Das Lehrkonzept hierfür wurde im Rahmen des Projekts Bi[professional] der Qualitätsoffensive Lehrerbildung entwickelt und durch den Qualitätsfonds für die Lehre der Universität Bielefeld gefördert.

2 Theoretischer Hintergrund der durchgeführten Maßnahme

2.1 Inverted Classroom (IC)

IC ermöglicht die Verlagerung der Wissensaneignung in die Selbstlernphase. So ist die Präsenzzeit im Seminar für „aktive", vertiefende und anwendungsorientierte Lerngelegenheiten geöffnet (LAGE, PLATT & TREGLIA, 2000). Wichtig ist hierbei, dass die Präsenzphase durch kognitiv höhere Aktivitäten, wie problemorientierte Arbeitsphasen, geprägt ist (vgl. WEIDLICH & SPANNAGEL, 2014). Die Dozierendenrolle wird eher als beratend, unterstützend und lernbegleitend beschrieben (vgl. BERGMANN & SAMS, 2012).

Ergebnisse zur Nützlichkeit von IC gegenüber klassischen Seminargestaltungen sind widersprüchlich (GIANNAKOS, KROGSTIE & SAMPSON, 2018). Studien verweisen auf positive Befunde (vgl. z. B. HUANG & HONG, 2016), nicht nachweisbare (z. B. CHEN, 2016) sowie negative Effekte (z. B. ARNOLD-GARZA, 2014).

Studien zur Nutzung von IC zur Didaktisierung forschungsmethodischer Lehre berichten positive Ergebnisse (BREITENBACH, 2016; STRAYER, 2012; WILSON, 2013). Als negativ wurde teilweise eine mangelnde Compliance der Studierenden und ihr Unverständnis über die Auslagerung der Inhalte auf die Selbstlernzeit festgestellt. Das diesem Werkstattbericht zugrunde liegende Konzept des Forschenden Lernens (HUBER, 2009) soll laut FREISLEBEN-TEUTSCHER (2018) durch IC und die damit verbundene Möglichkeit zum selbständigen Finden einer Fragestellung unterstützt werden.

2.2   Motivationale Begründung der Maßnahme

RYAN & DECI (2017) postulieren in der Self-Determination Theory (SDT), dass jeder Mensch das Bestreben hat, drei grundlegende psychologische Bedürfnisse zu erfüllen. Dies sind die Bedürfnisse nach Autonomie, Kompetenz und sozialer Eingebundenheit. Die Umgebung kann die Erfüllung der Grundbedürfnisse unterstützen und zwar durch die Lehrperson und das Lehr-Lern-Arrangement (RYAN & DECI, 2017). Die Wirkungskette von der Unterstützung der Grundbedürfnisse zu einem besseren Lernerfolg lässt sich folgendermaßen nachzeichnen: Die Unterstützung der Grundbedürfnisse führt zu ihrer wahrgenommenen Erfüllung (SKINNER & BELMONT, 1993). Die wahrgenommene Erfüllung der Grundbedürfnisse führt zu einer selbstbestimmten Form der Motivation (REEVE & JANG, 2006; RYAN & DECI, 2017). Selbstbestimmte Motivation führt zu stärkerem Engagement und besserer Leistung (REEVE, 2002; REEVE & JANG, 2006; RYAN & DECI, 2017).

IC sollte sich förderlich auf den Lernprozess im Allgemeinen und das Forschende Lernen der Studierenden im Speziellen auswirken, da er Möglichkeiten bietet, ihre Grundbedürfnisse zu erfüllen (vgl. FREISLEBEN-TEUTSCHER, 2018; SERGIS, SAMPSON & PELLICCIONE, 2018). Als Hauptpunkt ist die Flexibilisierung der Lehre zu nennen. Studierende können die methodischen Inhalte selbstgesteuert, in individueller Häufigkeit, Reihenfolge und Tiefe bearbeiten und sind dabei weder zeitlich noch räumlich gebunden (vgl. ARNOLD, KILIAN, THILLOSEN & ZIMMER, 2015). Diese Wahlfreiheit sollte als Teil von Autonomieförderung (KATZ & ASSOR, 2006) zu einer hohen wahrgenommenen Autonomie führen (vgl. REEVE & JANG, 2006). Zudem können Fragen und Interessen der Studierenden in der Präsenzzeit intensiver berücksichtigt werden. Auch dies ist Teil von Autonomieförderung (vgl. REEVE, 2002). Des Weiteren erlaubt IC eine Passung von Anforderungen und Fähigkeiten der Lernenden (LOVE et al., 2015), was eine Grundvoraussetzung für wahrgenommene Kompetenz ist (DANNER & LONKY, 1981). Durch die in der Präsenzsitzung frei werdende Zeit erhalten die Studierenden mehr individuelle Unterstützung, wodurch die Bedürfnisse nach Kompetenz und sozialer Eingebundenheit erfüllt werden sollten (vgl. SERGIS et al., 2018). Dies ist neben der Flexibilisierung der zweite große positive Aspekt der Neukonzeption als IC. Studien bestätigen die angenommene positive Wirkung von IC auf Motivation (BRAMLEY, 2018; KÜHL et al., 2017; SERGIS et al., 2018).

Übertragen auf das Forschende Lernen wird angenommen, dass Studierende nur dann eine Forschende Grundhaltung (FICHTEN, 2010a) entwickeln können, wenn sie mit ihrem Forschungsprozess zufrieden sind und sich nicht als methodisch inkompetent erleben (FICHTEN, 2010b). Misserfolgserlebnisse im Forschungsprozess aufgrund unprofessioneller Anleitung können zu Abneigung gegenüber Forschung führen (FICHTEN, 2010b).

3 Durchführung der Maßnahme IC

Durchgeführt wurde die Maßnahme im Sommersemester 2018 in zwei Vorbereitungsseminaren zum Praxissemester im Fach Biologie mit zwei unterschiedlichen

Lehrenden. Ein Seminar fungierte als Experimentalgruppe mit IC (N=16) und ein Seminar als Kontrollgruppe (KG) ohne IC (N=15).

Das Vorbereitungsseminar bestand aus zehn 90-minütigen Sitzungen (siehe Abb. 1). Am Ende dieses Blocks wurde die erste Version der Studienprojektskizze abgegeben. Die Dozierenden im IC und der KG zeigten allgemein ein grundbedürfnisförderliches Verhalten (vgl. RYAN & DECI , 2017), um ein gleichwertig unterstützendes Arbeitsklima aufzubauen.

Die ersten vier Sitzungen bestanden aus der Vermittlung fachdidaktischer Grundlagentheorien, die folgenden vier Sitzungen aus der Vermittlung forschungsmethodischer Inhalte. Diese Phase unterschied sich zwischen beiden Seminaren. Die KG-Sitzungen bestanden aus zwei 90-minütigen Vorträgen der Dozierenden zu quantitativen Forschungsmethoden. In den beiden jeweils darauffolgenden Sitzungen wurden Beispielstudien gelesen und dabei jeweils die gelernten Inhalte fokussiert sowie durch Leitfragen vertieft. Die Studierenden des IC hatten die Möglichkeit, in der Selbstlernzeit vorbereitend sechs bzw. fünf kurze Videos auf einer Lernplattform anzuschauen. Die Inhalte waren identisch zu den Vorträgen in der KG. Jede Videosequenz wurde mit einem Test in Form von Verständnisfragen mit Richtig/Falsch-Feedback abgeschlossen. In der ersten Sitzung nach den Videos bearbeiteten die Studierenden des IC die Beispielstudien entsprechend der KG. Die jeweils zweite Sitzung wurde mit kooperativen Methoden und der Hilfe des Dozierenden für Transfer und Anwendung der gelernten Inhalte auf die Studienprojekte genutzt. Beide Seminargruppen unterschieden sich nicht in den Lerngelegenheiten und dem tatsächlichen Workload, um Unterschiede zwischen den Gruppen plausibel auf IC zurückführen zu können. Dies wurde in der KG durch auf die jeweiligen Studienprojekte bezogene Reflektionsaufgaben in der Lernplattform gewährleistet. Zudem wurden der KG die Vortragsfolien sowie die Verständnisfragen analog zum IC als Nachbereitungsoption auf der Lernplattform angeboten. Die letzten beiden Sitzungen des Seminars wurden in beiden Gruppen für individuelle Beratung bezüglich der Studienprojekte verwendet.

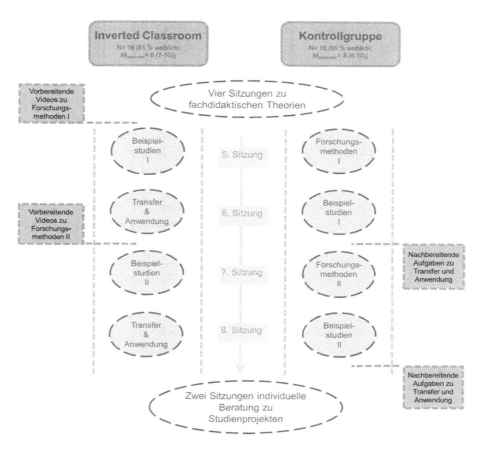

Abb. 1: Grafische Darstellung des Studiendesigns

4 Nutzen der Maßnahme als Open Educational Practice (OEP)

Mit dem vorgestellten Kurskonzept konnten, im Rahmen der institutionellen Möglichkeiten, lernförderliche Merkmale einer OEP adressiert werden (vgl. EHLERS,

2011). Um die Ausbildung der nötigen Kompetenzen ideal unterstützen zu können, wurde bei der Planung des Kurses Wert auf die Beachtung der Attribute einer Open Pedagogy von HEGARTY (2015) gelegt: Die Seminare (IC sowie KG) wurden durch die Möglichkeit des Austausches unter Studierenden und mit der Lehrperson auf einer digitalen Lernplattform ergänzt. Ebenso hatten die Studierenden die Möglichkeit, ihre fertigen Studienprojekte auf einer Plattform mit CC-Lizenz anderen Studierenden zur Verfügung zu stellen (*Attribut 1 participatory technologies*). Ein offener und vertrauensvoller Umgang wurde im Kurs erzeugt, indem die Dozierenden ein grundbedürfnisförderliches Verhalten zeigten und ihren Kurs dementsprechend strukturierten (*Attribut 2 openness and trust*). Eine konstruktivistische Kursgestaltung und die verwendeten kognitiv aktivierenden und kollaborativen Methoden sollten zudem eine innovationsförderliche Lernumgebung für die Studierenden schaffen, in der sie ihre eigenen Forschungsprojekte entwickeln konnten (*Attribut 3 innovation and creativity*). Die entwickelten IC-Videosequenzen und Reflexionsaufgaben werden als Open Educational Ressource (OER) unter einer CC-Lizenz für Dritte zur Verfügung gestellt. Hierbei wurde Wert auf den fachübergreifenden Nutzen gelegt. An der Universität Bielefeld wird ein Austauschportal (PortaBLe; https://uni-bielefeld.de/biprofessional/portaBLe/index.html) entwickelt, was unterschiedlichen Gruppen die Nutzung der IC-Videosequenzen ermöglichen wird: Dozierenden, Lehrkräften, aber auch Studierenden und außeruniversitären Lernenden. Dies ermöglicht die Nutzung im Sinne der Kriterien für „Open Content" (4Rs, WILEY, 2009; *Attribut 4 sharing ideas and ressources*). Eine „connected community" (*Attribut 5*) wurde durch die über zwei Semester konstante Kurszusammensetzung mit 1-2 Sitzungen pro Woche und kollaborativen Methoden erreicht. Ein Großteil der Forschungsprojekte wurde im IC in Gruppenarbeitsphasen im Austausch mit dem Dozierenden erarbeitet. Hierbei wurde auch die Möglichkeit der Publikation als OER auf der Plattform mit CC-Lizenz (http://www.bised.uni-bielefeld.de/praxisstudien/praxissemester/fo_le/steckbriefe) eröffnet (*Attribut 6 learner-generated content*). Das kooperative Arbeiten in der Präsenzzeit ermöglichte eine Reflektions- und Feedbackkultur (*Attribut 7 reflective practice*), welche sich positiv auf die Erfüllung der psychologischen Grundbedürfnisse der Studierenden auswirken und sie auch im folgenden Praxiskontakt zu einer Reflektion im

Handlungsfeld befähigen sollte. Die Veröffentlichung der IC-Videosequenzen, der Materialien und der didaktischen Aufbereitung des Seminars als OER soll durch die offene Zugänglichkeit Lehrende dabei unterstützen, diese wenig etablierten offenen Formate durch Peer-Review (*Attribut 8*) weiterzuentwickeln und sie in Universitäten fest zu integrieren.

5 Praxiserfahrungen und Forschungsperspektiven

Die antizipierten negativen Auswirkungen eines IC, z. B. mangelnde Compliance, konnten nicht festgestellt werden. Alle Studierenden des IC nutzten die Videosequenzen sowie Selbsttestaufgaben. Die Selbstlernzeit wurde also genutzt. Die subjektive Einschätzung des Dozierenden aus dem IC-Seminar bestätigt die Annahme, dass die Präsenzzeit somit für mehr Anwendungsfragen und problemorientierte Diskussionen genutzt werden konnte. Ebenso konnte der Dozierende eine zeitliche Entzerrung der Präsenzsitzungen feststellen. Die Ergebnisse für die KG zeigen hingegen, dass nur eine/r der 15 Studierenden die Möglichkeit der Abgabe der freiwilligen Reflexionsaufgaben zum Transfer auf das eigene Studienprojekt genutzt hat. Die freiwillig bearbeitbaren Verständnisfragen haben im Schnitt drei Studierende bearbeitet. Folglich hat sich die effektive Lernzeit der Studierenden des IC erhöht. Die methodische Umsetzung durch IC kann daher insgesamt als vorteilhaft beschrieben werden. Eine mögliche Ursache für die unterschiedliche Nutzung der Materialien könnte in der subjektiven Relevanz der Inhalte liegen. Die KG nutzte die Selbstlernzeit vermutlich nicht, da sie auch ohne die Bearbeitung der Aufgaben den Präsenssitzungen folgen konnte. Somit wurden die Vertiefungsaufgaben der Selbstlernphasen möglicherweise als unnötiger Aufwand eingestuft. Die Studierenden des IC hingegen mussten die Aufgaben bearbeiten, um effektiv in den Präsenzterminen mitarbeiten zu können. Dies könnte andeuten, unter welchen Umständen es bei IC zu Compliance-Problemen kommen kann.

In einem Vor-/Nachtest-Interventions-Design wurde die Maßnahme quantitativ evaluiert (vgl. BASTEN, SCHUMACHER & MERTENS, 2019). Die Ergebnisse zur Erfüllung der Grundbedürfnisse zeigen keine Unterschiede der beiden Gruppen bezüglich wahrgenommener Kompetenz ($t(1;28)=1.98$, $p=.06$) und Autonomie ($t(1;28)=0.51$, $p=.62$). Ein signifikanter Unterschied ergab sich bei der sozialen Eingebundenheit zugunsten des IC ($t(1;28)=2.35$, $p=.03$, $d=.85$). Eine mögliche Erklärung ist die stärker kooperativ gestaltete Präsenzzeit im IC. Die Lehrperson übernahm eine Beraterrolle und agierte auf einer Ebene mit den Lernenden. Zusätzlich ist die vermehrte individuelle Kontaktzeit zwischen Dozierenden und Studierenden zu nennen, welche eine stärkere soziale Eingebundenheit gefördert haben könnte. Um die Befunde der Evaluation genauer zu ergründen, wurden im nächsten Schritt qualitative Interviews geführt. Zudem können die verfassten Studienprojekte und Ergebnisse der Reflektionsprüfung beider Gruppen hinsichtlich ihrer Qualität verglichen werden.

6   Literaturverzeichnis

Arnold, P., Kilian, L., Thillosen, A. M. & Zimmer, G. M. (2015). *Handbuch E-Learning* (4. erweiterte Aufl.). Bielefeld: W. Bertelsmann Verlag.

Arnold-Garza, S. (2014). The Flipped Classroom Teaching Model and Its Use for Information Literacy Instruction. *Communications in Information Literacy, 8*(1), 7-22.

Basten, M., Schumacher, F. & Mertens, C. (2019). Methodische Vorbereitung auf das Studienprojekt im Praxissemester – Vergleich eines Inverted-Classroom-Ansatzes mit Präsenzlehre. In J. Kosinár, A. Gröschner & U. Weyland (Hrsg.), *Langzeitpraktika als Lernräume – Historische Bezüge, Konzeptionen und Forschungsbefunde* (S. 175-188). Münster: Waxmann.

Bergmann, J. & Sams, A. (2012). *ASCD Webinars – Flipped Classroom Webinar Series*. http://www.scoop.it/t/teaching-innovation, Stand vom 14. Februar 2019.

Bramley, G. (2018). How to help engage students in flipped learning: a flipping eventful journey. *Student Engagement in Higher Education Journal, 2*(1), 78-85.

Breitenbach, A. (2016). Teaching Statistics with the Inverted Classroom Model. *International Journal of Innovation and Research in Educational Sciences, (3)*4, 2349-5219.

Chen, L. L. (2016). Impacts of flipped classroom in high school health education. *Journal of Educational Technology Systems, 44*(4), 411-420.

Danner, F. W. & Lonky, E. (1981). A cognitive-developmental approach to the effects of rewards on intrinsic motivation. *Child Development, 52*(3), 1043-1052.

Ehlers, U.-D. (2011). Extending the territory: From open educational resources to open educational practices. *Journal of Open, Flexible and Distance Learning, 15*(2), 1-10.

Fichten, W. (2010a). Forschendes Lernen in der Lehrerbildung. In U. Eberhard (Hrsg.), *Neue Impulse in der Hochschuldidaktik* (S. 127-182). Berlin: Springer.

Fichten, W. (2010b). Konzepte und Wirkungen forschungsorientierter Lehrerbildung. In J. Abel & G. Faust (Hrsg.), *Wirkt Lehrerbildung? Antworten aus der empirischen Forschung* (S. 271-281). Münster: Waxmann.

Freisleben-Teutscher, C. (2018). Das Format des Inverted Classroom in der Praxis. In J. Lehmann & H. A. Mieg (Hrsg.), *Forschendes Lernen* (S. 214-227). Potsdam: Verlag der Fachhochschule Potsdam.

Giannakos M. N., Krogstie J. & Sampson D. (2018). Putting Flipped Classroom into Practice: A Comprehensive Review of Empirical Research. In D. Sampson, D. Ifenthaler, J. M. Spector & P. Isaías (Hrsg.), *Digital Technologies: Sustainable Innovations for Improving Teaching and Learning* (S. 27-44). Cham: Springer.

Großmann, N., Fries, S. & Wilde, M. (im Druck). Forschendes Lernen in der Biologiedidaktik (Humanbiologie/Zoologie). In M. Basten, C. Mertens & E. Wolf (Hrsg.), Forschendes Lernen in Bielefeld: Fachdidaktische Profile. *PFLB-PraxisForschungLehrer*innenBildung.*

Hegarty, B. (2015). Attributes of Open Pedagogy: A Model for Using Open Educational Resources. *Educational Technology, 55*(4), 3-13.

Huang, Y. N. & Hong, Z. R. (2016). The effects of a flipped English classroom intervention on students' information and communication technology and English reading comprehension. *Educational Technology Research and Development, 64*(2), 175-193.

Huber, L. (2009). Warum Forschendes Lernen nötig und möglich ist. In L. Huber, J. Hellmer & F. Schneider (Hrsg.), *Forschendes Lernen im Studium. Aktuelle Konzepte und Erfahrungen* (S. 9-36). Bielefeld: UVW.

Katz, I. & Assor, A. (2006). When Choice Motivates and When It Does Not. *Educational Psychology Review, 19*(4), 429-442.

Kühl, S., Toberer, M., Kreis, O., Tolks, D., Fischer, M.R. & Kühl, M. (2017). Konzeption und Nutzen der Inverted Classroom-Methode für eine kompetenzorientierte Biochemie Lehrveranstaltung im vorklinischen Studienabschnitt der Humanmedizin. *GMS Journal for Medical Education, 34*(3), 1-27.

Lage, M. J., Platt, G. J. & Treglia, M. (2000). Inverting the classroom: A gateway to creating an inclusive learning environment. *The Journal of Economic Education, 31*(1), 30-43.

Love, B., Hodge, A., Corritore, C. & Ernst, D.C. (2015). Inquiry-Based Learning and the Flipped Classroom Model. *PRIMUS, (25)*8, 745-762.

MSW (Ministerium für Schule und Weiterbildung des Landes NRW) (2010). Rahmenkonzeption zur strukturellen und inhaltlichen Ausgestaltung des Praxissemesters im lehramtsbezogenen Masterstudiengang.

Reeve, A. (2002). Self-determination theory applied to educational settings. In R. M. Ryan & E. L. Deci (Hrsg.), *Handbook of self-determination research* (S. 183-203). Rochester, NY: University of Rochester Press.

Reeve, J. & Jang, H. (2006). What teachers say and do to support students' autonomy during a learning activity. *Journal of Educational Psychology, 98*(1), 209-218.

Riewerts, K., Weiß, P., Wimmelmann, S., Saunders, C., Beyerlin, S., Gotzen, … Gess, C. (2018). Forschendes Lernen entdecken, entwickeln, erforschen und evaluieren. *die hochschullehre, 4*/2018, 389-406.

Ryan, R. M. & Deci, E. L. (2017). *Self-Determination Theory – Basic Psychological Needs in Motivation, Development, and Wellness.* New-York: Guilford Press.

Sergis, S., Sampson, D. G. & Pelliccione, L. (2018). Investigating the impact of Flipped Classroom on students' learning experiences: A Self-Determination Theory approach. *Computers in Human Behavior, 78*, 368-378.

Skinner, E. A. & Belmont, M. J. (1993). Motivation in the classroom: Reciprocal effects of teacher behavior and student engagement across the school year. *Journal of Educational Psychology, 85*(4), 571-581.

Strayer, J. F. (2012). How learning in an inverted classroom influences cooperation, innovation and task orientation. *Learning Environments Research, 15*(2), 171-193.

Weidlich, J. & Spannagel, C. (2014). Die Vorbereitungsphase im Flipped Classroom. Vorlesungsvideos versus Aufgaben. In K. Rummler (Hrsg.), *Lernräume gestalten – Bildungskontexte vielfältig denken* (S. 237-248). Münster: Waxmann.

Wiley, D. (2009). Defining "Open". http://opencontent.org/blog/archives/1123, Stand vom 14. Februar 2019.

Wilson, S. (2013). The Flipped Class: A Method to Address the Challenges of an Undergraduate Statistics Course. *Teaching of Psychology, 40*(3), 193-199.

Werkstattbericht

Autor/innen

Fabian SCHUMACHER ‖ Universität Bielefeld, Fakultät für Biologie – Biologiedidaktik und Sachunterrichtsdidaktik ‖ Universitätsstraße 25, D-33615 Bielefeld

https://ekvv.uni-bielefeld.de/pers_publ/publ/
PersonDetail.jsp?personId=84654613

fschumacher@uni-bielefeld.de

Dr. Claudia MERTENS ‖ Universität Bielefeld, Fakultät für Erziehungswissenschaften ‖ Universitätsstraße 25, D-33615 Bielefeld

https://ekvv.uni-bielefeld.de/pers_publ/publ/
PersonDetail.jsp?personId=108299896

claudia.mertens@uni-bielefeld.de

Dr. Melanie BASTEN ‖ Universität Bielefeld, Fakultät für Biologie – Sachunterrichtsdidaktik ‖ Universitätsstraße 25, D-33615 Bielefeld

https://ekvv.uni-bielefeld.de/pers_publ/publ/
PersonDetail.jsp?personId=11411346

melanie.basten@uni-bielefeld.de